AUTHENTIC GUITAR TAB EDITION

MYTUNES 4x4 SERIES

Hard Rock Guitar TAB

D0864026

Alfred Publishing Co., Inc.
16320 Roscoe Blvd., Suite 100
P.O. Box 10003
Van Nuys, CA 91410-0003
alfred.com

ISBN-10: 0-7390-5814-2
ISBN-13: 978-0-7390-5814-5

Cover photograph courtesy of FotoSets.

CONTENTS BY ARTIST

CONTENTS BY SONG

THE CLINCHER

Lyrics by
PETE LOEFFLER
Music by
CHEVELLE

*All gtrs. in Drop D, down 2 steps:
⑥ = B♭ ③ = E♭
⑤ = F ② = G
④ = B♭ ① = C

Moderately slow ♩ = 88

Intro:

N.C.

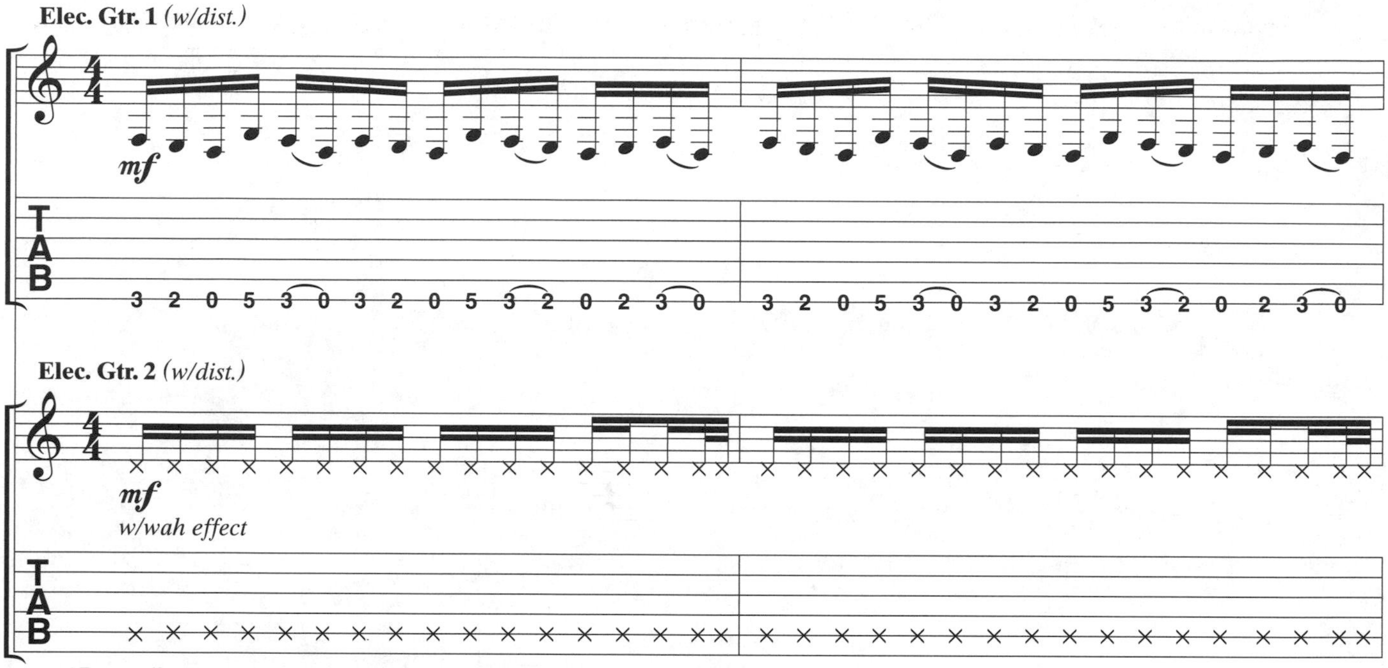
Elec. Gtr. 1 (w/dist.)
mf
3 2 0 5 3 0 3 2 0 5 3 2 0 2 3 0
3 2 0 5 3 0 3 2 0 5 3 2 0 2 3 0
Elec. Gtr. 2 (w/dist.)
mf
w/wah effect

*Recording sounds two whole steps lower than written.

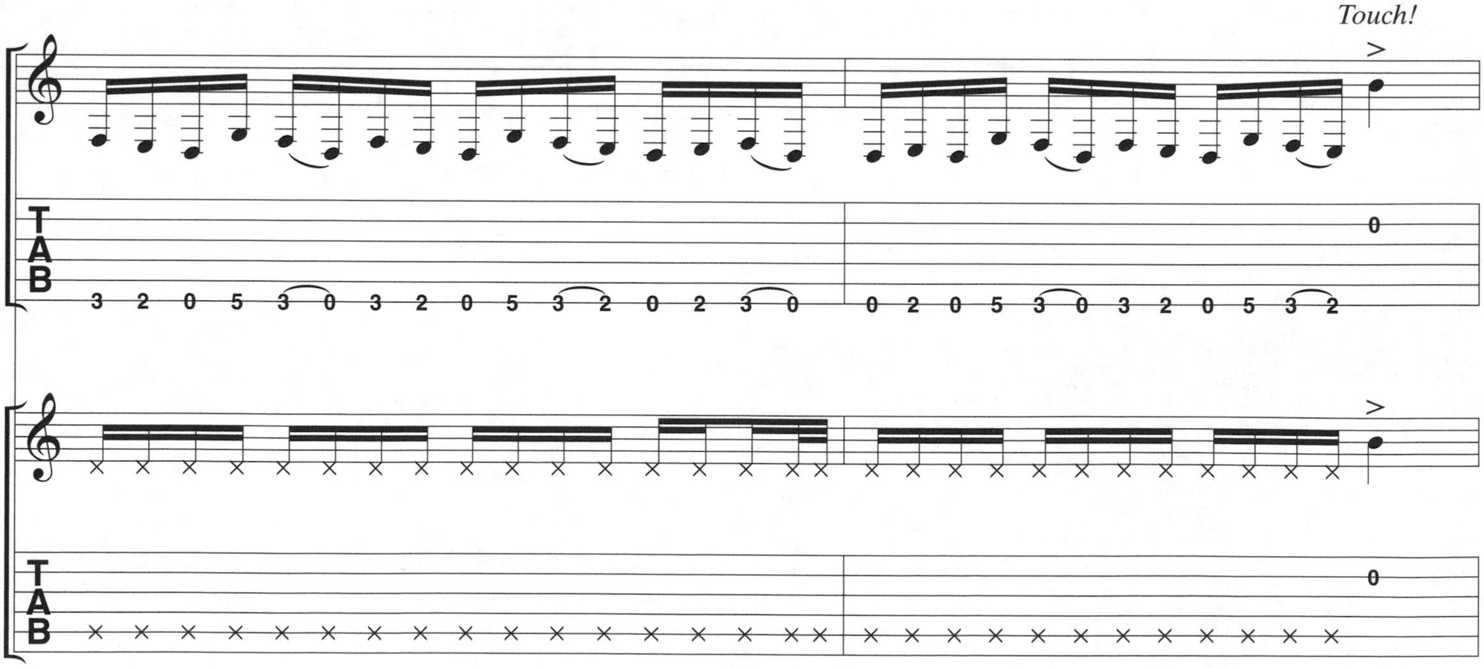
Touch!
3 2 0 5 3 0 3 2 0 5 3 2 0 2 3 0
0 2 0 5 3 0 3 2 0 5 3 2
0
0

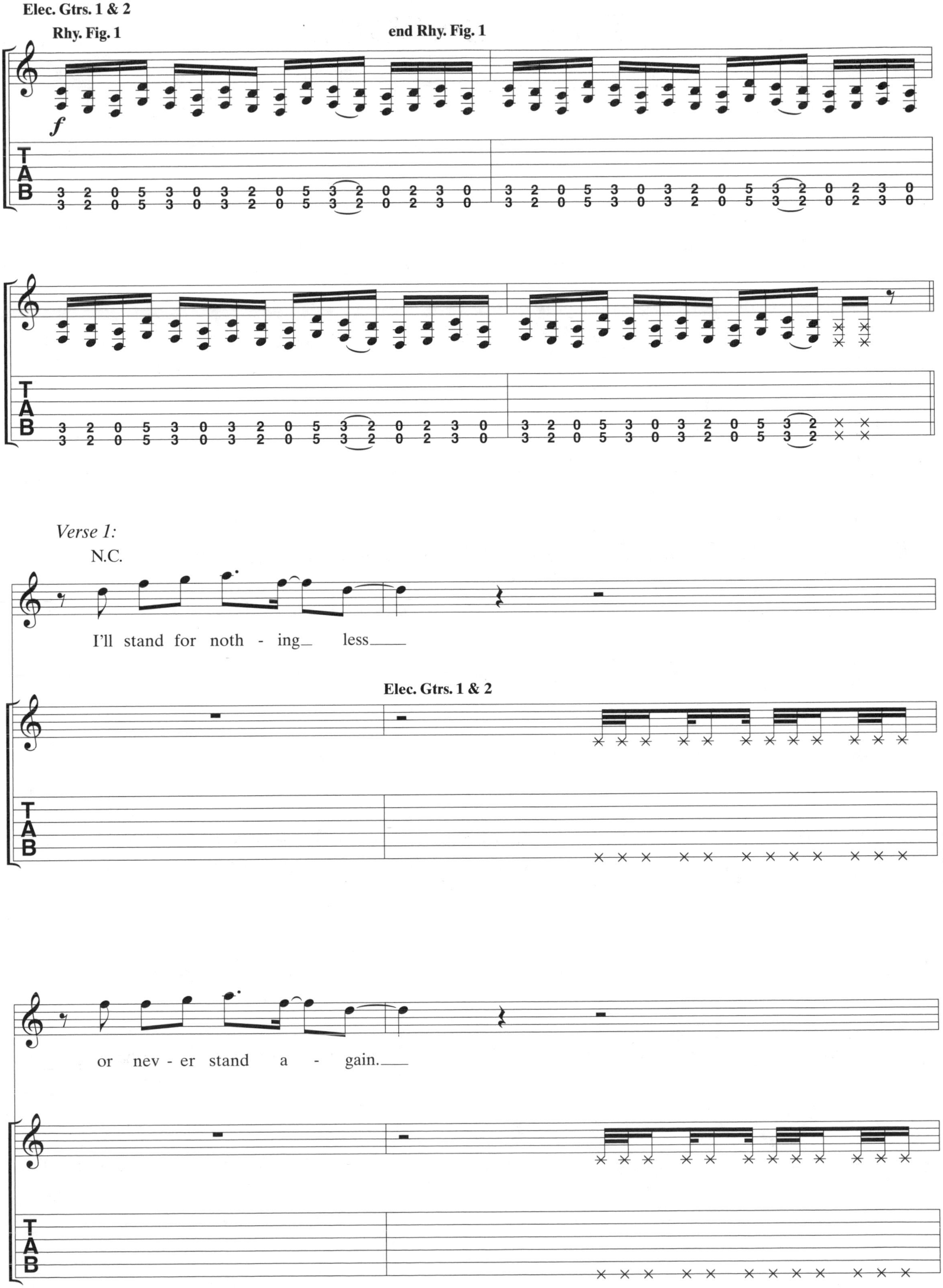
Elec. Gtrs. 1 & 2
Rhy. Fig. 1
end Rhy. Fig. 1
f
Verse 1:
N.C.
I'll stand for noth - ing less
Elec. Gtrs. 1 & 2
or nev - er stand a - gain.

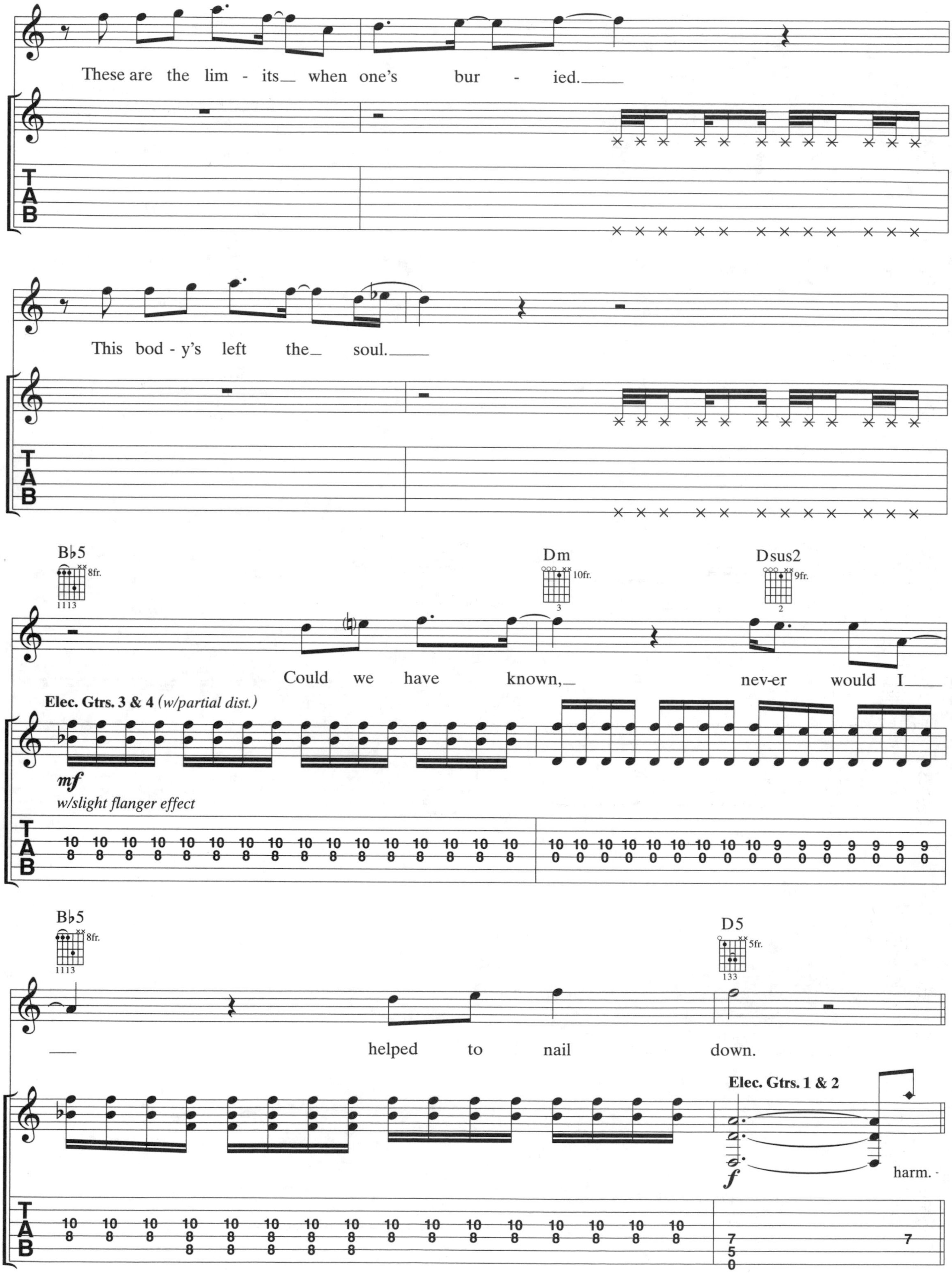
These are the lim - its when one's bur - ied.
This bod - y's left the soul.
B♭5
8fr.
1113
Dm
10fr.
3
Dsus2
9fr.
2
Could we have known, nev-er would I
Elec. Gtrs. 3 & 4 (w/partial dist.)
mf
w/slight flanger effect
B♭5
8fr.
1113
D5
5fr.
133
helped to nail down.
Elec. Gtrs. 1 & 2
f
harm.

Care - ful of drift - ing off,
Rhy. Fig. 2
end Rhy. Fig. 2
harm.
T
A
B
7
0
7
w/Rhy. Fig. 2 (*Elec. Gtrs. 1 & 2) 3 times, simile
now los - ing taste and touch.
Turn - ing a pale blue,
*Composite arrangement.
lean - ing in to say
this bod - y's left the soul.
D5
E♭5
C5
5fr.
6fr.
3fr.
133
Elec. Gtrs. 1 & 2
Vocals dbld. 8vb
The brain needs ox - y - gen.
Cont. rhy. simile
Can't sneak a - round this bait,
his cat - a - comb has got me by the chin.

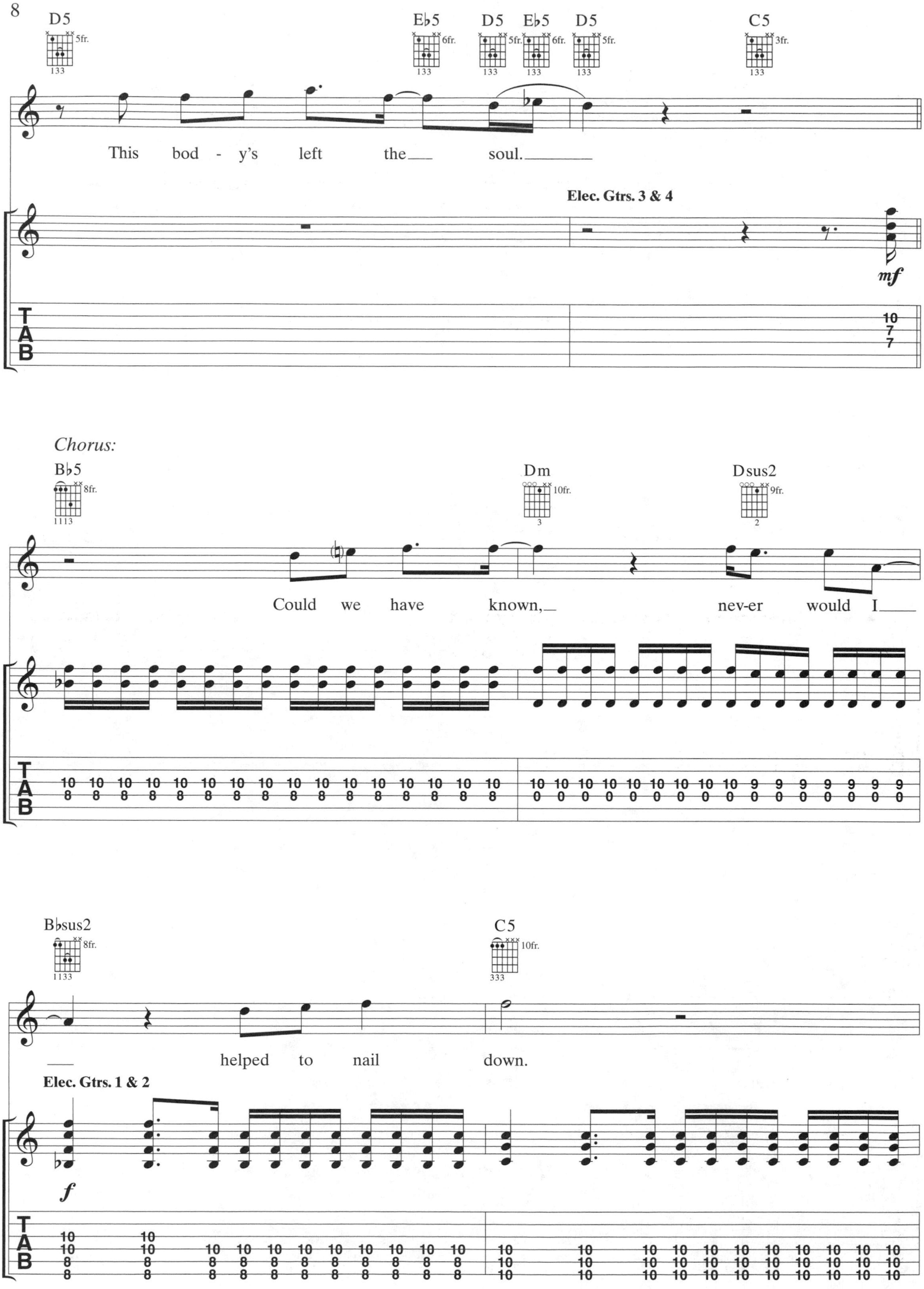
D5
Eb5
D5
Eb5
D5
C5
This bod - y's left the soul.
Elec. Gtrs. 3 & 4
mf
Chorus:
Bb5
Dm
Dsus2
Could we have known, nev-er would I
Bbsus2
C5
helped to nail down.
Elec. Gtrs. 1 & 2
f

B♭5
Dm
Dsus2
With noth - ing to gain,
here's the clinch - er;
F5
C5
this should be you.
Now sat - u - rate,
Elec. Gtr. 2 cont. in slashes
Chorus:
D5
Elec. Gtr. 2
now sat - u - rate,
now sat - u - rate,
Elec. Gtr. 1
P.M.

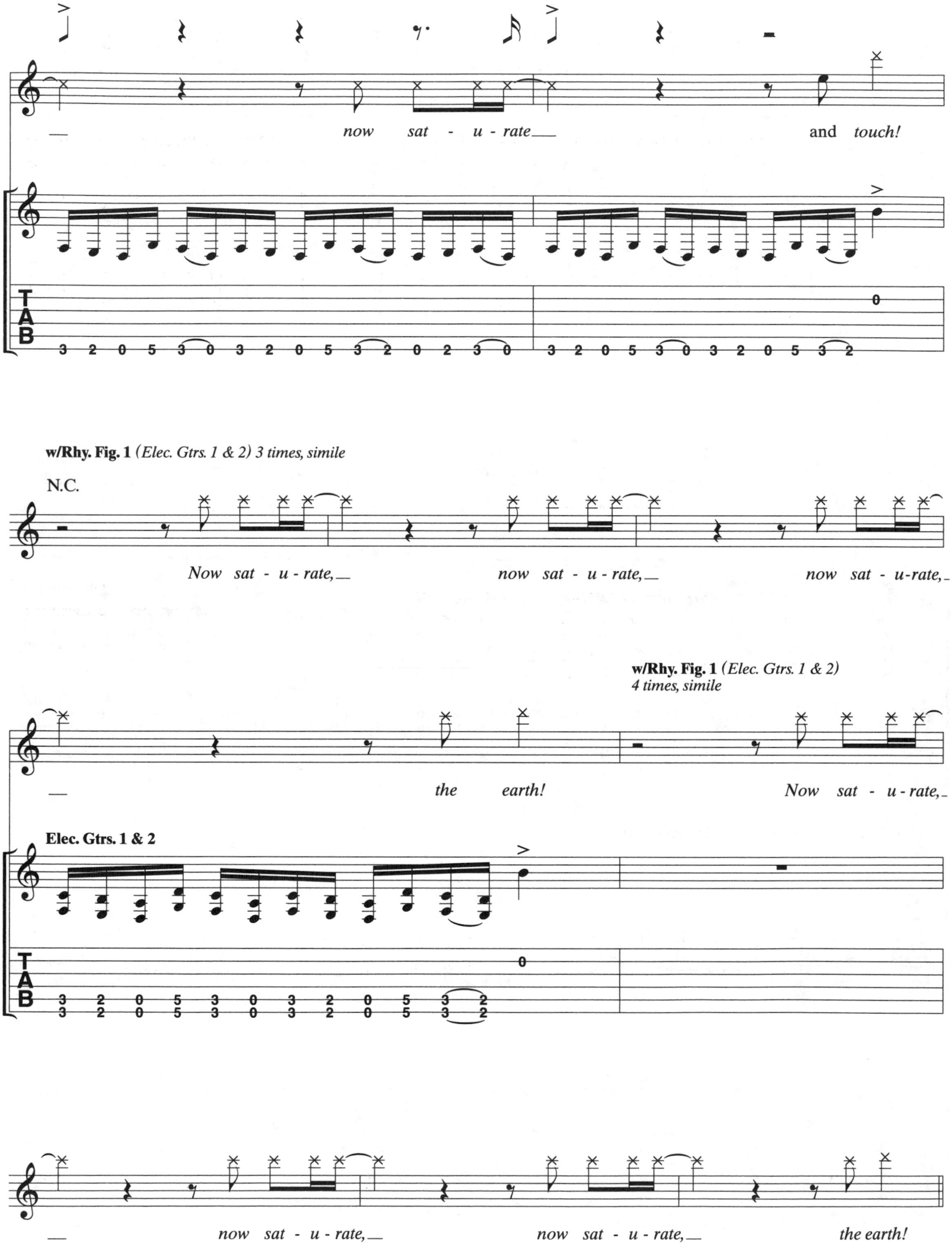
now sat - u - rate
and touch!
w/Rhy. Fig. 1 (Elec. Gtrs. 1 & 2) 3 times, simile
N.C.
Now sat - u - rate,
now sat - u - rate,
now sat - u-rate,
the earth!
w/Rhy. Fig. 1 (Elec. Gtrs. 1 & 2) 4 times, simile
Now sat - u - rate,
Elec. Gtrs. 1 & 2
now sat - u - rate,
now sat - u - rate,
the earth!

Chorus:
B♭5
8fr.
1113
Dm
10fr.
3
Dsus2
9fr.
2
Elec. Gtrs. 1 & 2
Rhy. Fig. 3
How, could we have known,___ nev-er would I___
Fsus2
3fr.
111341
C5
3fr.
133
___ helped to nail___ down.
Bkgd. Vocal: Stand for noth - ing_ lost.
end Rhy. Fig. 3
w/Rhy. Fig. 3 (Elec. Gtrs. 1 & 2) 4 times, simile
With noth-ing to gain,___ here's_ the clinch - er;___ this should be you._
___ Made cold and crip - pled._ This hap-pened to be___ nev-er chang - ing,_

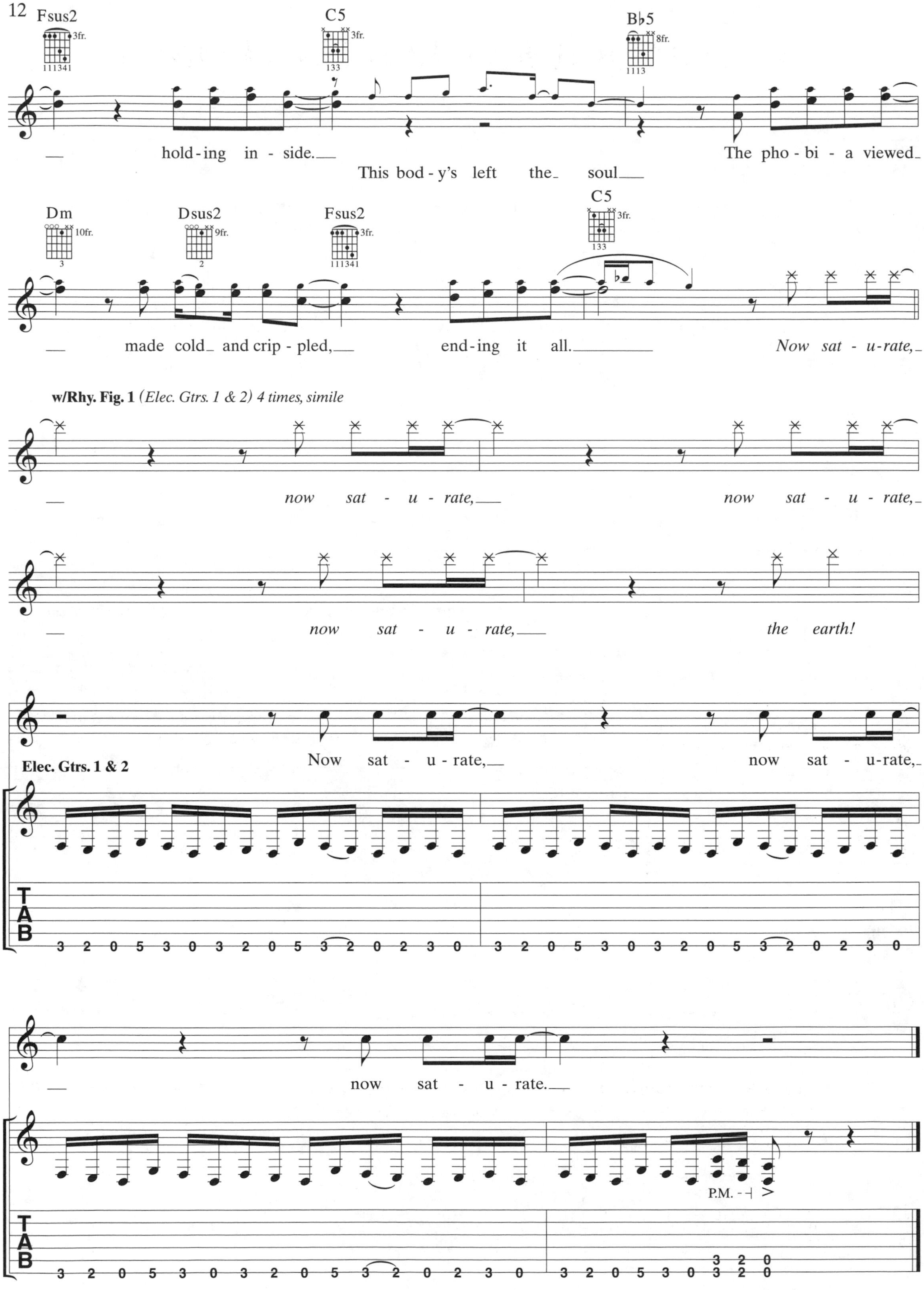
Fsus2
3fr.
111341
C5
3fr.
133
B♭5
8fr.
1113
hold-ing in-side.
This bod-y's left the soul
The pho-bi-a viewed
Dm
10fr.
3
Dsus2
9fr.
2
Fsus2
3fr.
111341
C5
3fr.
133
made cold and crip-pled,
end-ing it all.
Now sat-u-rate,
w/Rhy. Fig. 1 (Elec. Gtrs. 1 & 2) 4 times, simile
now sat-u-rate,
now sat-u-rate,
now sat-u-rate,
the earth!
Now sat-u-rate,
now sat-u-rate,
Elec. Gtrs. 1 & 2
TAB
now sat-u-rate.
P.M.
TAB

VITAMIN R (LEADING US ALONG)

*All gtrs. in Drop D, down 1 1/2 steps:
⑥ = B ③ = E
⑤ = F♯ ② = G♯
④ = B ① = C♯

Lyrics by
PETE LOEFFLER
Music by
CHEVELLE

Slowly ♩. = 63 (♪ = 189)

Intro:
D2
D5
D2
Elec. Gtr. 1 (w/dist.)
mf
hold throughout
*Recording sounds a minor third lower than written.
Verse:
D5
Dm
D(2)
1. Some will learn; man - y do,
2. Af - ter all, what's the point?
Elec. Gtrs. 1 & 2 (w/dist.)
Rhy. Fig. 1
P.M. throughout
Dm
D(2)
B♭5
8fr.
1113
cov - er up or spread it out. Turn a - round,
'Cause lev - i - ta - tion is pos - si - ble if you're a fly.

Bb5(b5)
Bb5
Bb5(b5)
8fr.
had e - nough,
pick and choose
or pass it
A - chieved and gone,
there's time for this
and so much
end Rhy. Fig. 1
w/Rhy. Fig. 1 (Elec. Gtrs. 1 & 2) simile
Dm
D(2)
on. Buy - ing in,
head - ing for
suf - fer now
or suf - fer
more. It's typ - i - cal
cre - ate a world,
a spe - cial place of my de -
then. It's bad e - nough,
I want the fear,
need the fear
'cause he's a -
sign. to nev - er cope
or nev - er care.
Just use the key
'cause he's a -
Pre-chorus:
F
lone.
lone.
Bkgd. Vocals: He has be - come.
Elec. Gtrs. 1 & 2

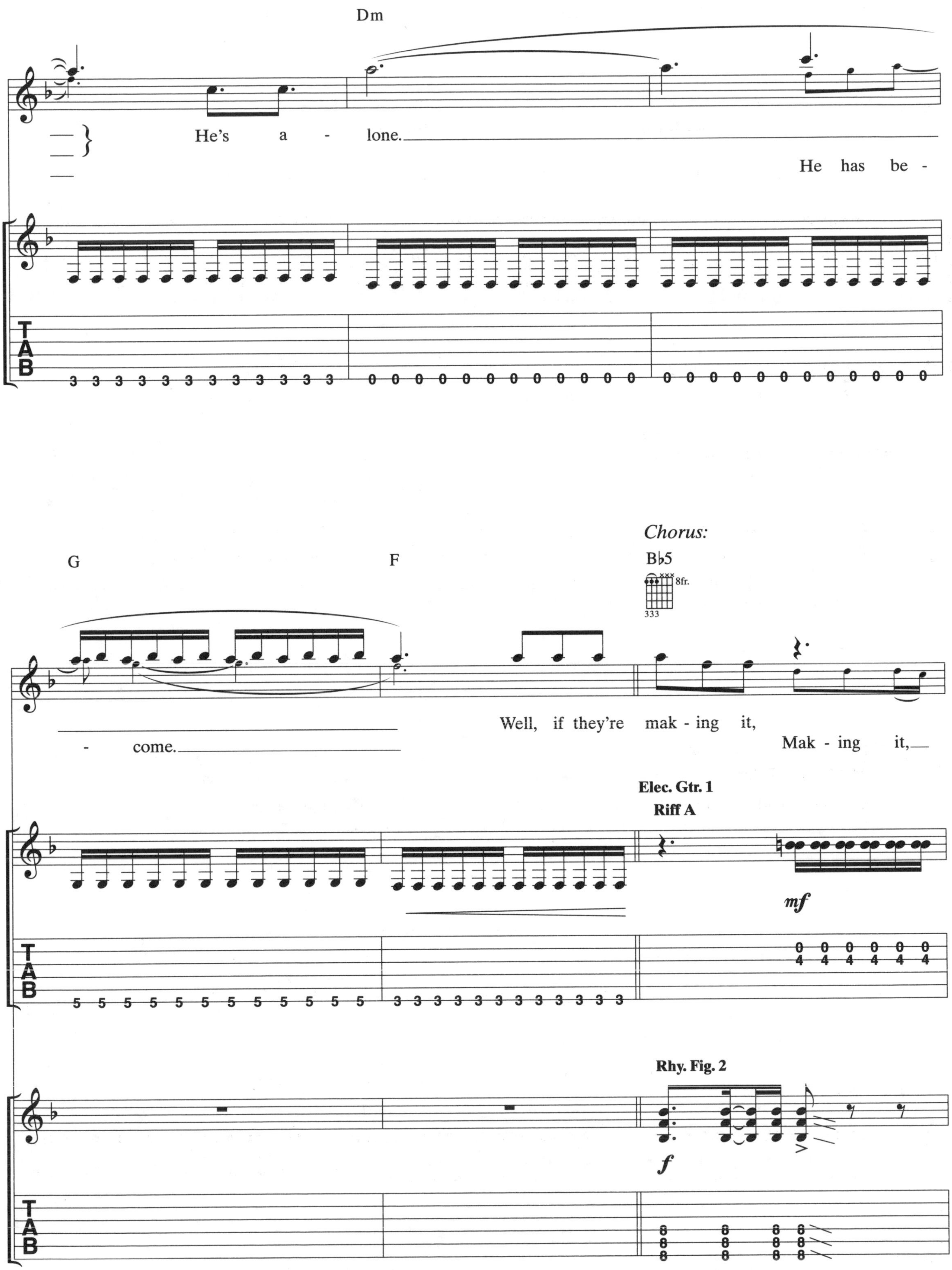
Dm
He's a - lone.
He has be -
Chorus:
G
F
Bb5
8fr.
333
- come.
Well, if they're mak - ing it,
Mak - ing it,
Elec. Gtr. 1
Riff A
mf
Rhy. Fig. 2
f
TAB

C5
10fr.
G5
5fr.
F5
crush - ing it, lead - ing us a - long. The
crush - ing it.
end Riff A
end Rhy. Fig. 2
w/Rhy. Fig. 1 (Elec. Gtr. 2) simile
w/Riff A (Elec. Gtr. 1) simile
B♭5
8fr.
C5
10fr.
G5
5fr.
1.
F5
has - sle of the scream - ing fits that pan - ic makes, re - morse.
The has - sle of scream - ing fits.
D5
Elec. Gtr. 2
Elec. Gtr. 1
hold throughout

2.
Bridge:
F5 D5 G5 D5 D5
morse.
O - ver and o - ver a slave.
Elec. Gtrs. 1 & 2
F5 D5 G5 D5 D5
Be - came o - ver and o - ver a slave.
B♭5 D5 G5 D5 D5
Be - came o - ver and o - ver a slave.

Interlude:
B♭5
D5
G5
D5
D5
Be - came_ o - ver and_ o - ver a slave.
Elec. Gtr. 1
Elec. Gtr. 2
Well, if they're

Chorus:
w/Rhy. Fig. 1 (Elec. Gtr. 2) 2 times, simile
w/Riff A (Elec. Gtr. 1) 2 times, simile
B♭5 8fr. 333
C5 10fr. 333
G5 5fr. 333
F5 333
mak - ing it, crush - ing it, lead - ing us a - long. The
Mak - ing it, crush - ing it.
B♭5 8fr. 333
C5 10fr. 333
G5 5fr. 333
1.
F5 333
has - sle of the scream - ing fits that pan - ic hell be - fore. Well, if they're
pan - ic makes re -
The has - sle of scream - ing fits.
2.
Outro:
D5 13
Elec. Gtr. 2
morse!
Elec. Gtr. 1
TAB
Start slow fade
Fade

*All gtrs. in Drop D, tuned down 2 whole steps:
⑥ = B♭ ③ = E♭
⑤ = F ② = G
④ = B♭ ① = C

I GET IT

Music by
CHEVELLE
Words by
PETE LOEFFLER

Moderately ♩ = 124

Intro:

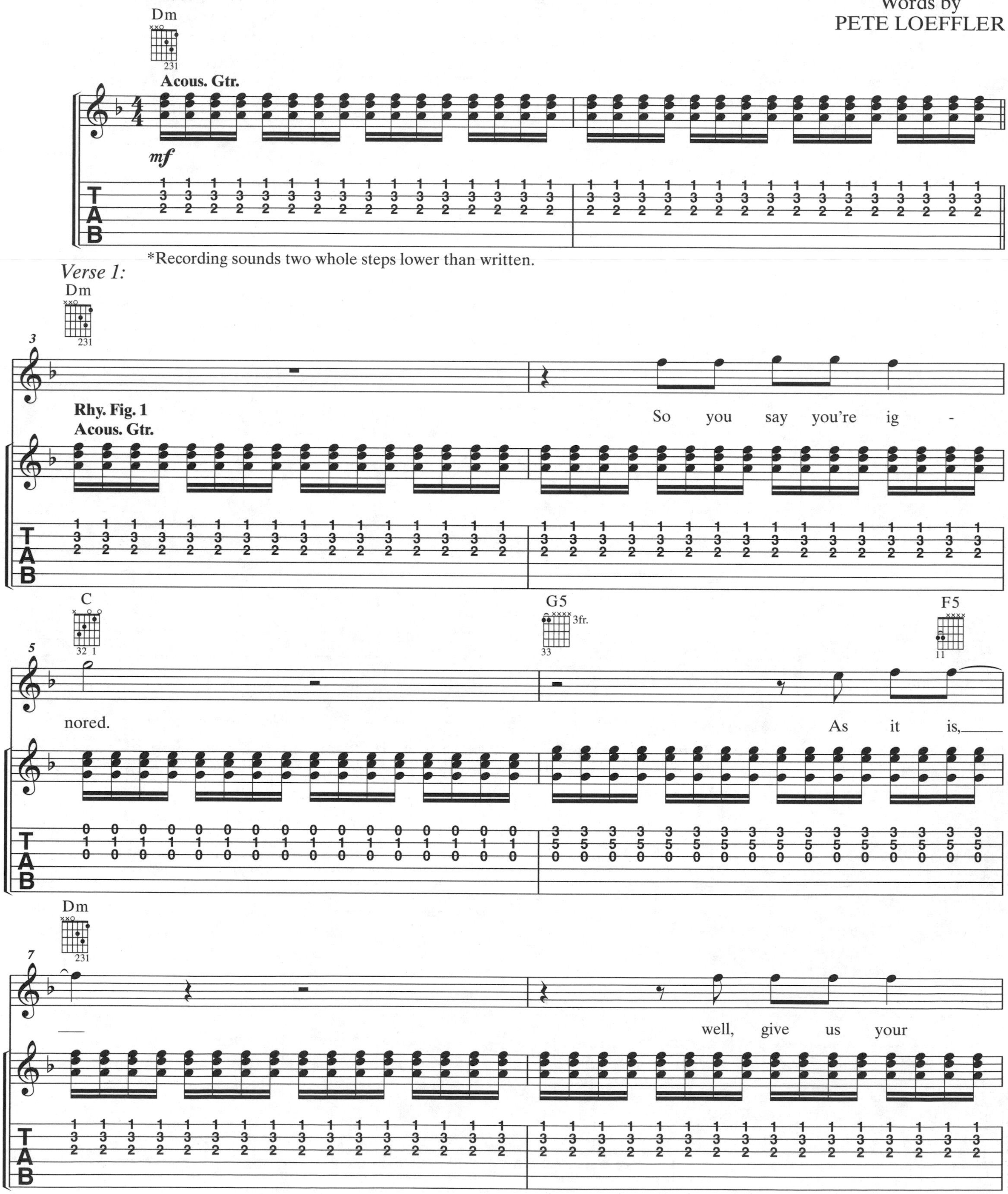

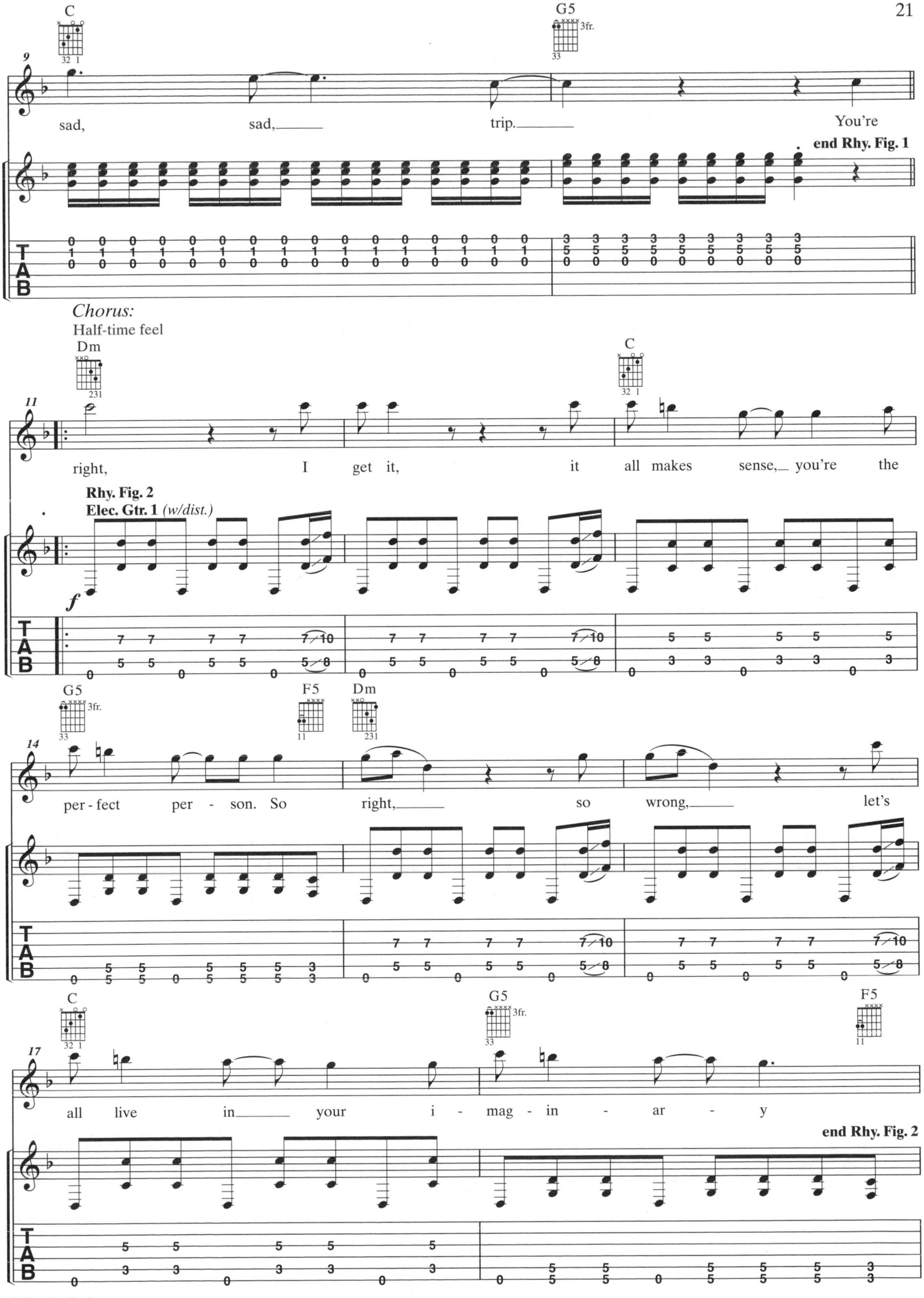
C
G5
sad, sad, trip. You're
end Rhy. Fig. 1
Chorus:
Half-time feel
Dm
C
right, I get it, it all makes sense, you're the
Rhy. Fig. 2
Elec. Gtr. 1 (w/dist.)
G5
F5
Dm
per - fect per - son. So right, so wrong, let's
C
G5
F5
all live in your i - mag - in - ar - y
end Rhy. Fig. 2

end half-time feel
Dm
231
19
life.
Acous. Gtr.
Elec. Gtr. 1
hold
21
2. As
3. Press
hold

Verses 2 & 3:
Dm C G5 F5
w/Rhy. Fig. 1 (Acous. Gtr.) 1st 4 meas. only, 2 times
sumed it's wheth - er we're right___ or wrong.___ We're___
on these tan - nins, they'll dou - ble in time.___ The touch of
Elec. Gtr. 2 (clean-tone w/tremolo)
mf
(2nd time only)
Dm C G5 F5
doomed,_ and there's plen - ty for all._______ 1. How
life,_____ once failed to men - tion so___ far. 2. Of
Pre-chorus:
w/Rhy. Fig. 1 (Acous. Gtr.)
Dm C
dare you catch__ me count - ing, how dare you call___ at
course the law___ is foun - tains, or face to face___ re -
Elec. Gtr. 3 (w/light dist.)
mf

G5 F5 Dm
all. How dare you call it suf - f'ring, how
morse. A fast and rest - less black - mail like
C
1. G5 F5
2. G5 F5
dare you call at all. You're force. You're
pent - up fet - ish
Chorus:
Half-time feel
Dm C
right, I get it, it all makes sense, you're the
Elec. Gtr. 1
G5 F5 Dm
per - fect per - son. So bright, so wrong, let's

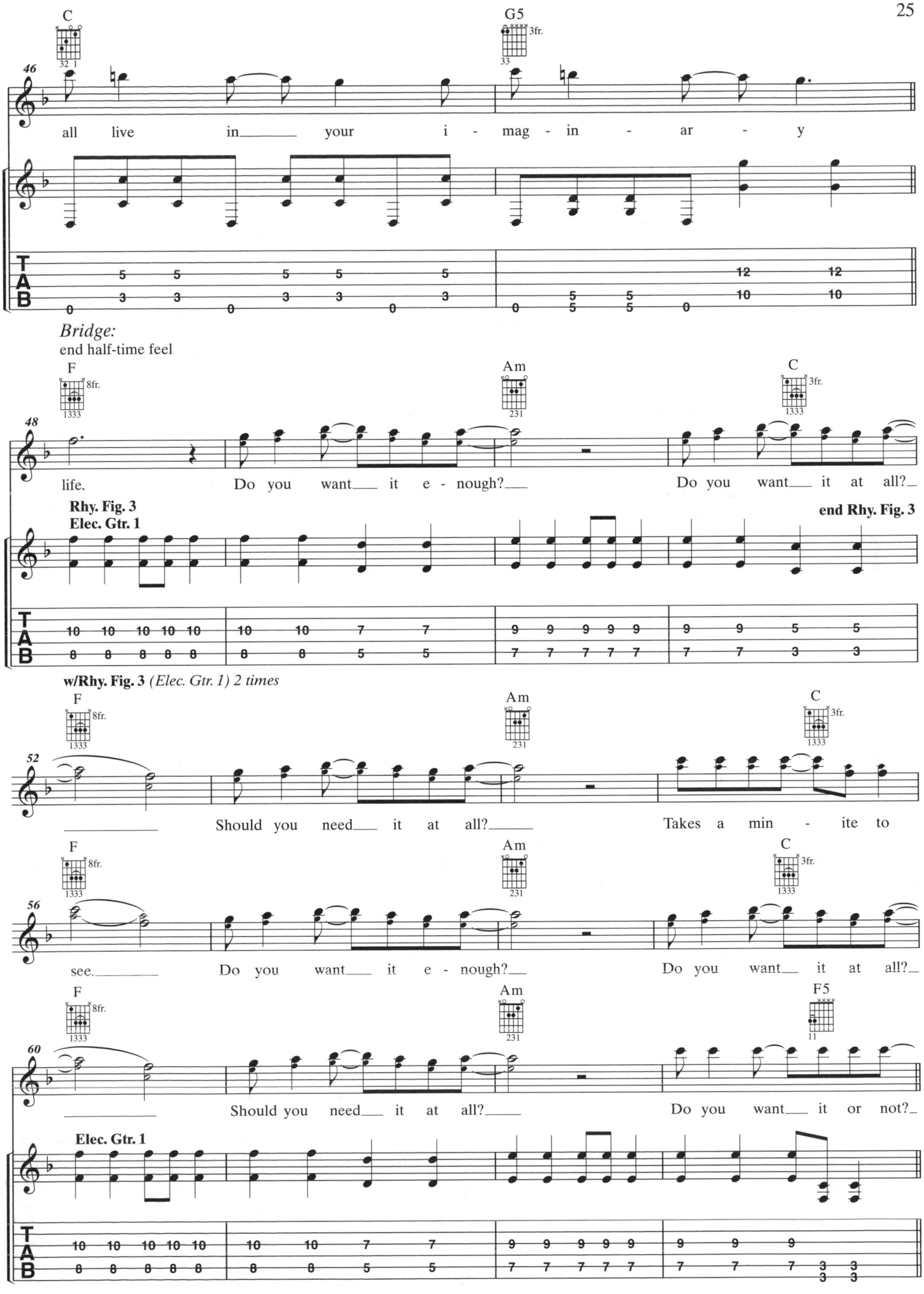
C
G5
46
all live in___ your i - mag - in - ar - y
Bridge:
end half-time feel
F
Am
C
48
life. Do you want___ it e - nough?___ Do you want___ it at all?_
Rhy. Fig. 3
Elec. Gtr. 1
end Rhy. Fig. 3
w/Rhy. Fig. 3 (Elec. Gtr. 1) 2 times
52
___ Should you need___ it at all?___ Takes a min - ite to
56
see.___ Do you want___ it e - nough?___ Do you want___ it at all?_
F5
60
___ Should you need___ it at all?___ Do you want___ it or not?_
Elec. Gtr. 1

Interlude:

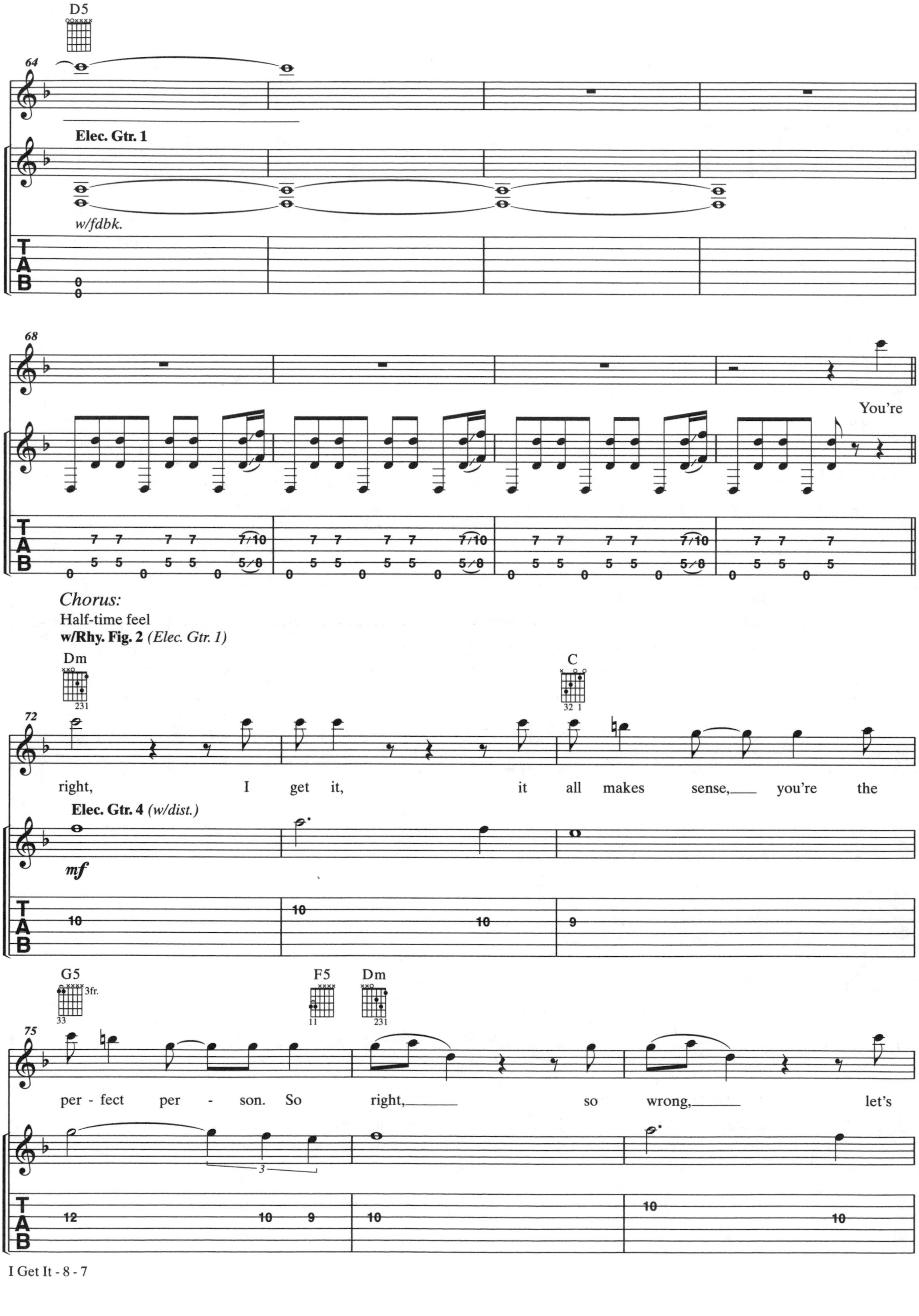
D5
64
Elec. Gtr. 1
w/fdbk.
TAB
68
You're
Chorus:
Half-time feel
w/Rhy. Fig. 2 (Elec. Gtr. 1)
Dm
C
72
right, I get it, it all makes sense, you're the
Elec. Gtr. 4 (w/dist.)
mf
G5
3fr.
F5
Dm
75
per - fect per - son. So right, so wrong, let's

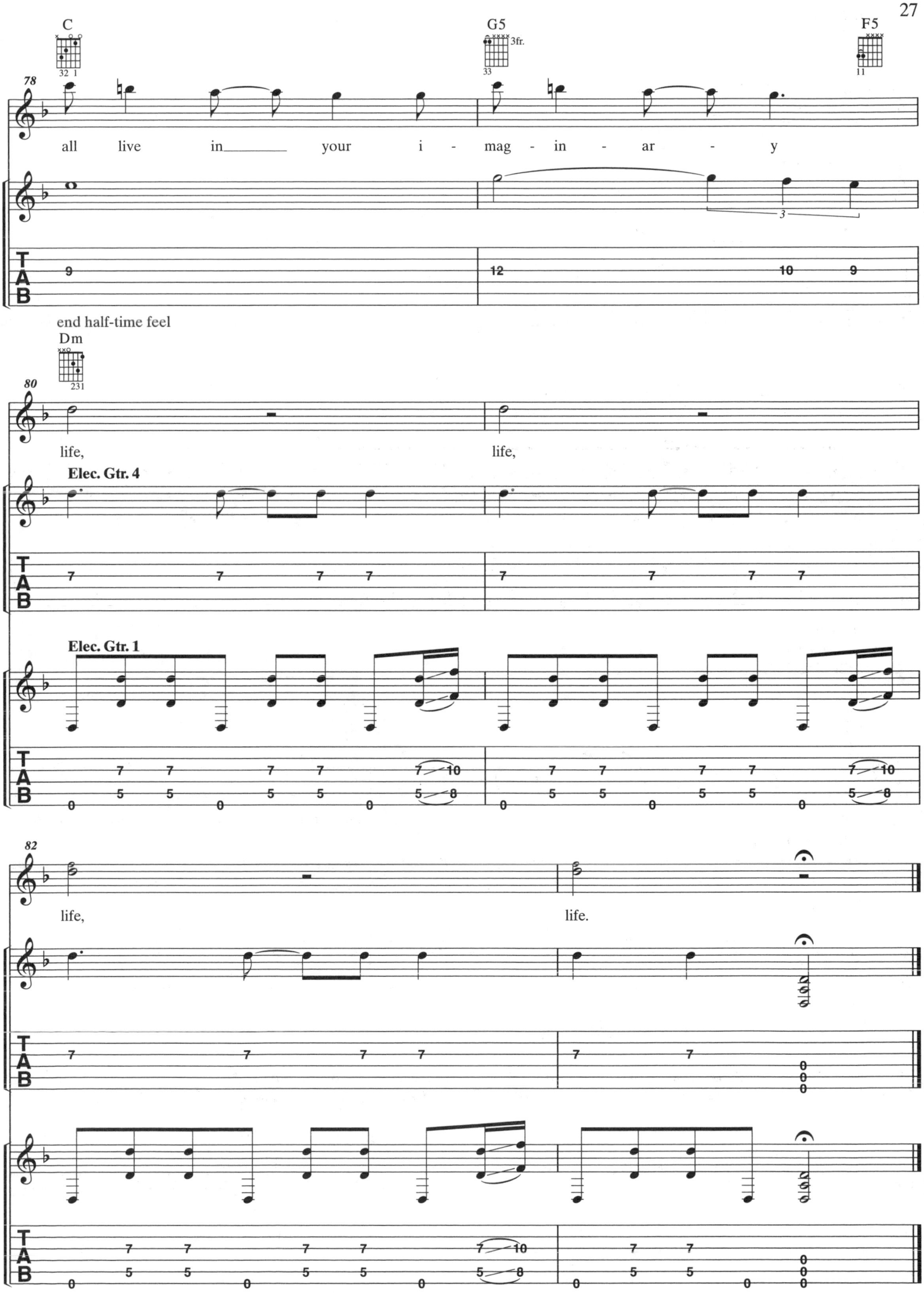
C
G5
3fr.
F5
all live in your i - mag - in - ar - y
end half-time feel
Dm
life,
life,
Elec. Gtr. 4
Elec. Gtr. 1
life,
life.

SEND THE PAIN BELOW

Words by PETE LOEFFLER
Music by CHEVELLE

*All gtrs. in Drop D, down 1 1/2 steps:

⑥ = B ③ = E
⑤ = F♯ ② = G♯
④ = B ① = C♯

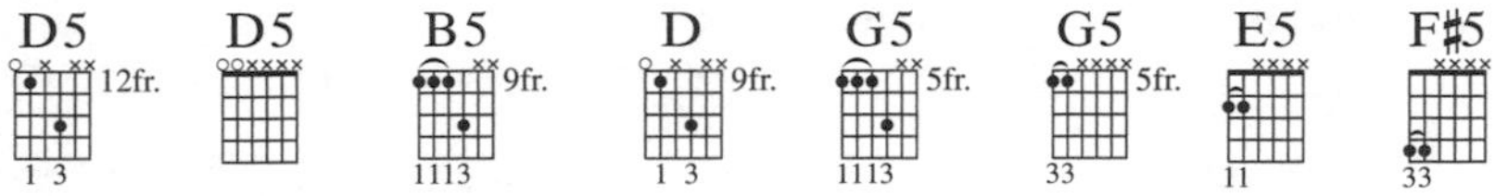

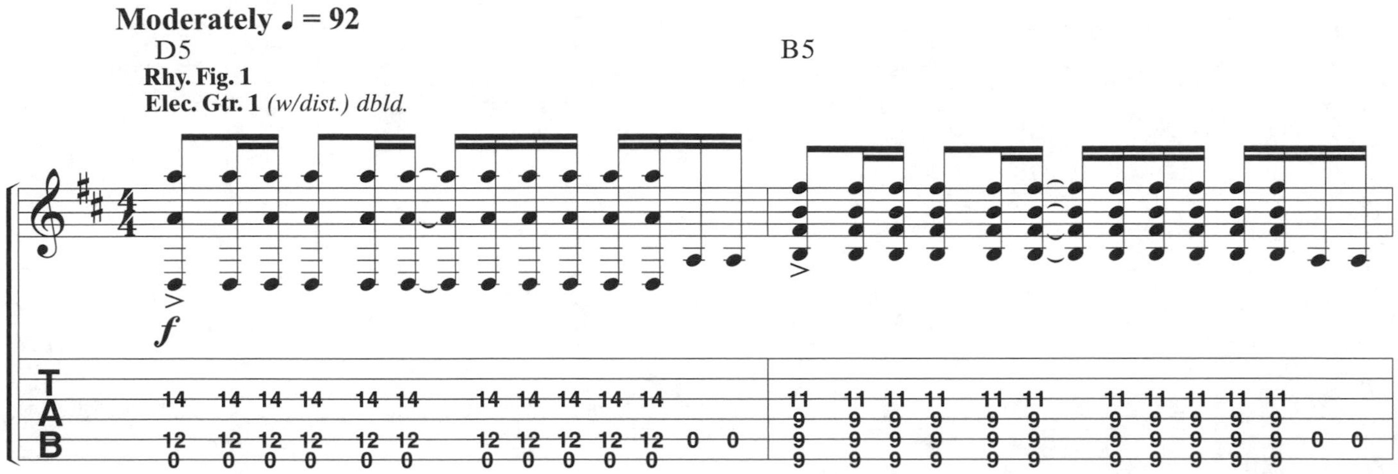

*Music sounds a min. 3rd lower than written.

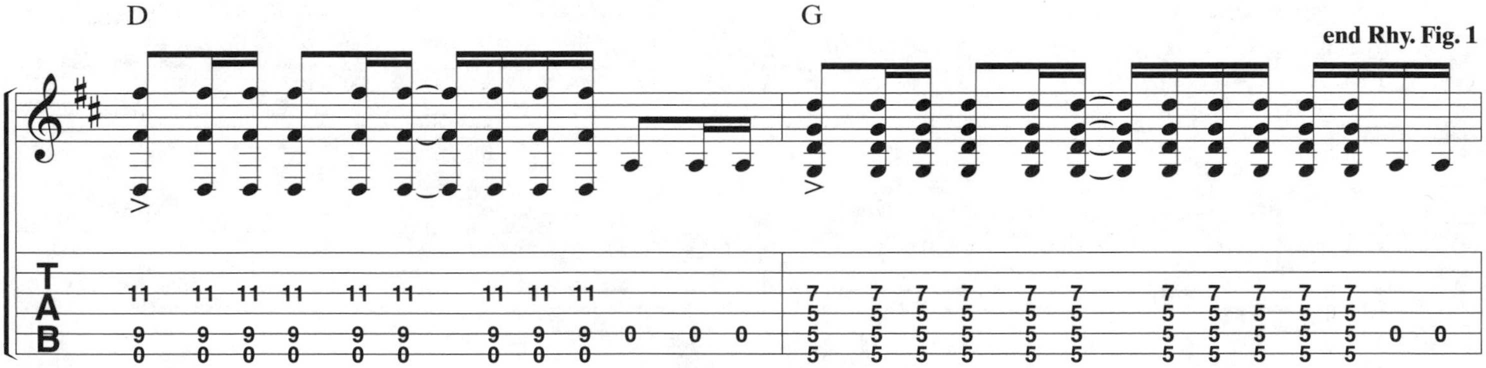

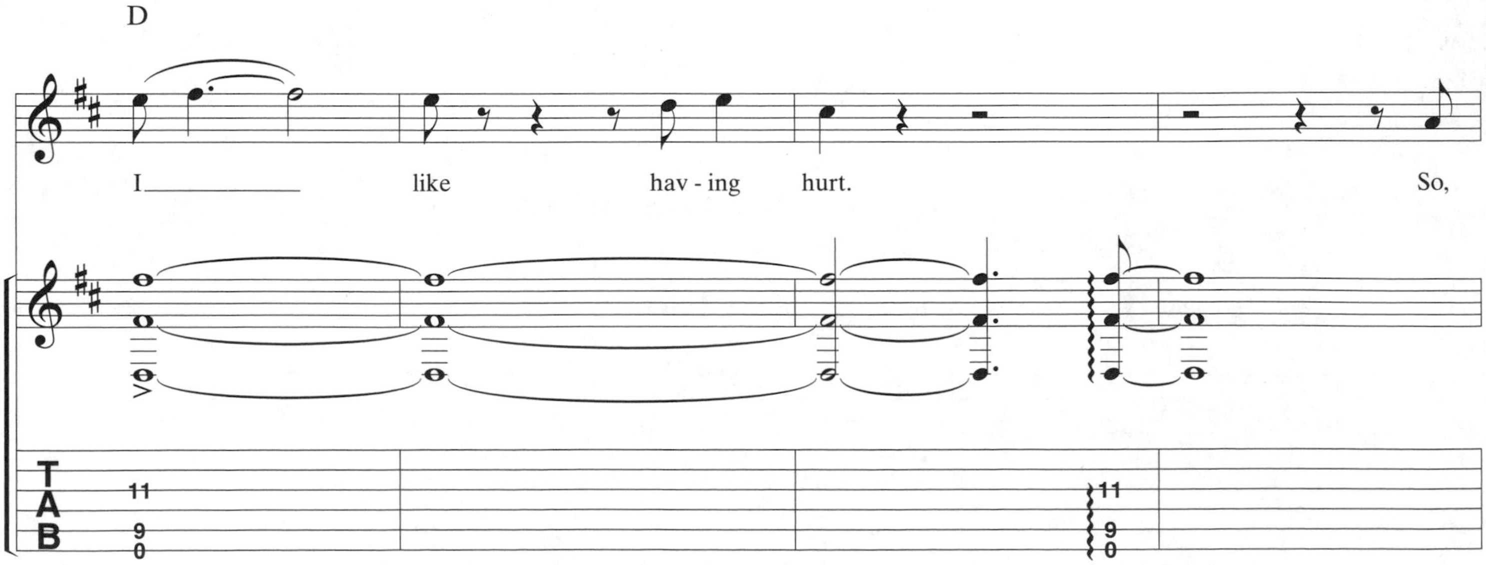

send the pain be - low where I need it
1. You used to
Verse:
D
D/F♯*
beg me to take care of things
run me a - way all while laugh -
Rhy. Fig. 2
Elec. Gtr. 1 (clean-tone)
end Rhy. Fig. 2
*F♯ played by bass gtr. only.
w/Rhy. Fig. 2 (Elec. Gtr. 1) 3 times, simile
D D/F♯* D D/F♯*
ing
and smile at the thought of me fail -
then cry a - bout that fact 'til I re -
Pre-chorus:
w/Rhy. Fig. 1 (Elec. Gtr. 1, clean-tone) 2 times, simile
D D/F♯* D5 B5
- ing.
- turned.
But long be - fore hav - ing
D G5 D5 B5
hurt
I'd send the pain be - low,
I'd

Chorus:
w/Rhy. Fig. 1 (Elec. Gtr. 1 w/dist.)
2 times, simile
D
G5
D5
send the pain be - low. Much like suf - fo - cat - ing,
B5
D
G5
much like suf - fo - cat - ing, much like suf - fo - cat - ing,
2ndVcl.: I'd
D
B5
D
much like suf - fo - cat - ing.
send the pain be - low, I'd send the pain be - low.
1.
2.
Bridge:
G5
G5
D5 E5
D5
G5
D5
2. You used to much like suf - fo - cat - ing.
Elec. Gtr. 1 (clean-tone)
E5
D5
G5
F♯5
D5 E5
D5
G5
D5
I can't feel my chest, chest,
Rhy. Fig. 3
Elec. Gtr. 1 (w/dist.) dbld.

w/Rhy. Fig. 3 (Elec. Gtr. 1 dbld.) 4 times, simile
E5 D5 G5 F♯5
D5 E5 D5 G5 D5 E5 D5G5 F♯5
chest an-y - more.__ Drop__ down, clos-ing in.__
end Rhy. Fig. 3
trem. picking
D5 E5 D5 G5 D5 E5 D5 G5 F♯5 D5 E5 D5 G5 D5 E5 D5 G5 F♯5 D5 E5 D5 G5 D5
I can't feel my chest. Drop down.
E5 D5 G5 F♯5 N.C.
Outro Chorus:
w/Rhy. Fig. 1 (Elec. Gtr. 1 dbld.) 2 times, simile
D5 B5
I like hav - ing__
sendthepainbelow- . Much like suf - fo - cat - ing.__
Elec. Gtr. 1 (w/dist.)
steady gliss.
trem. picking
D G5 D5 B5
hurt. So send the pain__ be - low,____ so
Sendthe painbe - low. Muchlikesuf - fo - cat - ing. Muchlikesuf - fo - cat - ing.
D
1. G5
2. G5
D
Elec. Gtr. 1 (dbld.)
send the pain__ be - low.__ Much like suf-fo-cat - ing. __
2ndVcl.: So,

FAR AWAY

*All gtrs. in Drop D, down 1/2 step:
⑥ = D♭ ③ = G♭
⑤ = A♭ ② = B♭
④ = D♭ ① = E♭

Lyrics by CHAD KROEGER
Music by NICKELBACK

Moderately slow ♩ = 84
Intro:

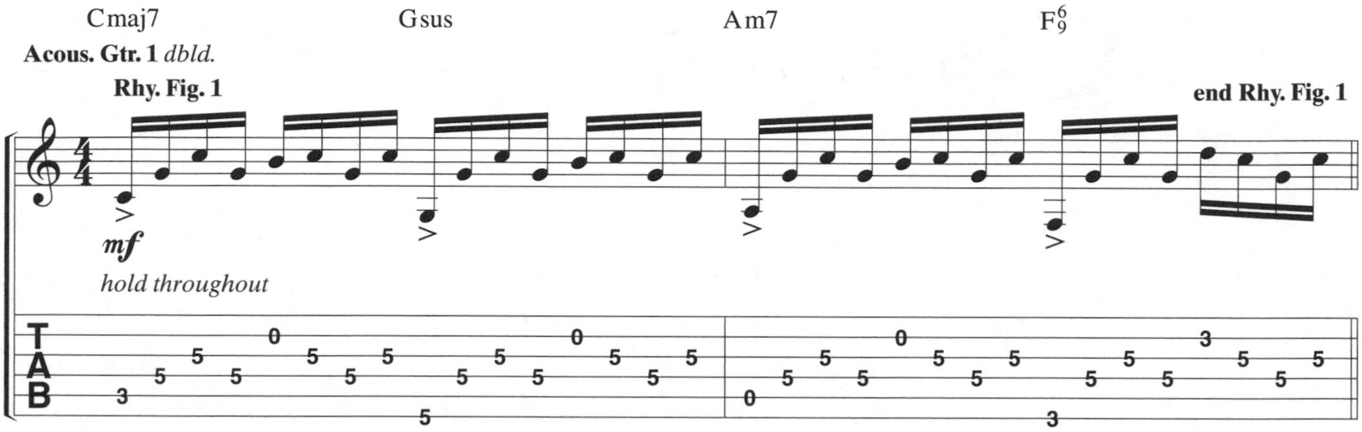

*Recording sounds a half step lower than written.

Verse:
w/Rhy. Fig. 1 *(Acous. Gtr. 1) 3 times, simile*

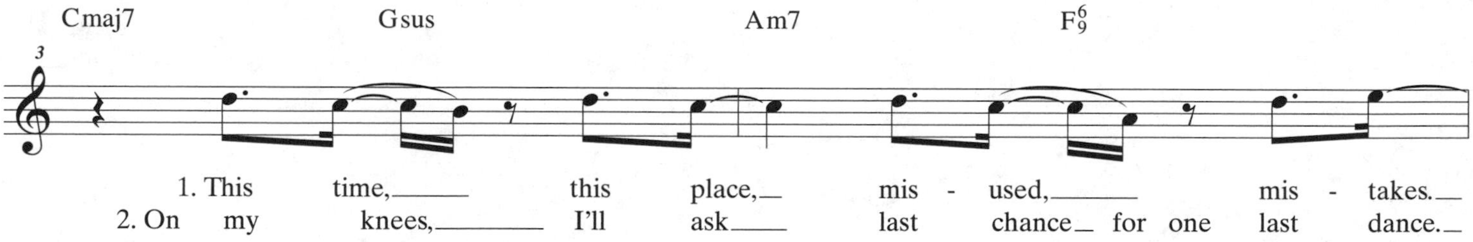
Cmaj7
Gsus
Am7
F6/9
3
1. This time, this place, mis - used, mis - takes.
2. On my knees, I'll ask last chance for one last dance.

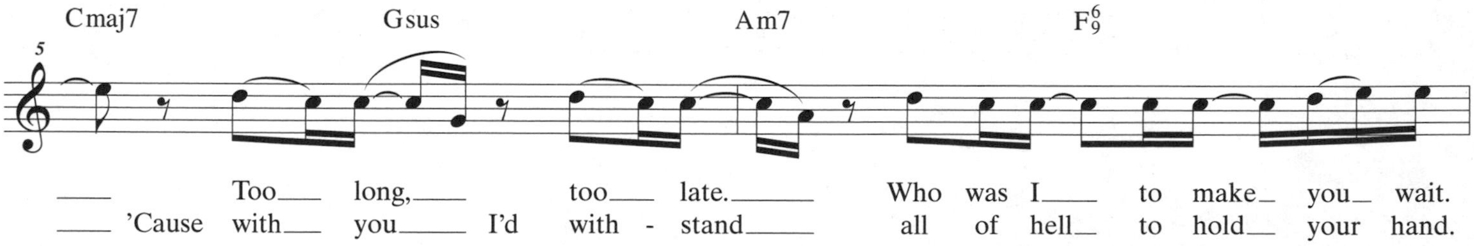
Cmaj7
Gsus
Am7
F6/9
5
Too long, too late. Who was I to make you wait.
'Cause with you I'd with - stand all of hell to hold your hand.

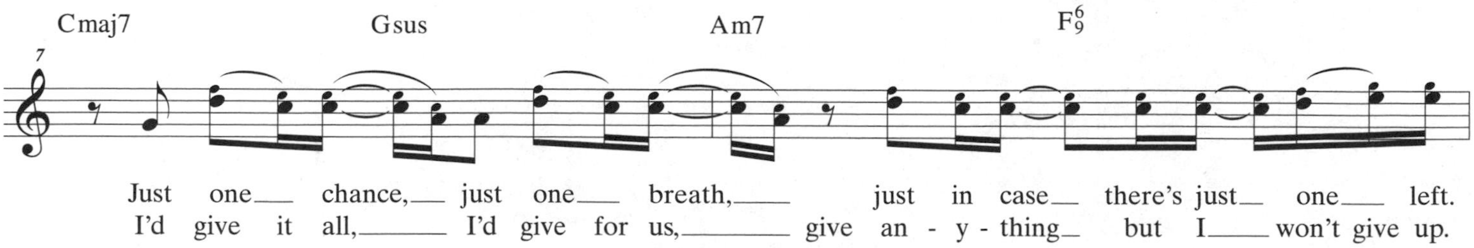
Cmaj7
Gsus
Am7
F6/9
7
Just one chance, just one breath, just in case there's just one left.
I'd give it all, I'd give for us, give an - y - thing but I won't give up.

Dsus2
F6/9
'Cause you know, you know, you know.
'Cause you know, you know, you know.
Ah.
Acous. Gtr. 1
hold throughout
Chorus:
C
G5
Am
Fmaj7
Acous. Gtr. 1 dbld.
I love you,
I have loved you all along.
Elec. Gtr. 1 (clean-tone)
Riff A
end Riff A
mf
hold throughout
Cont. simile
C
G5
Am
Fmaj7
And I miss you,
been far away for far too long.

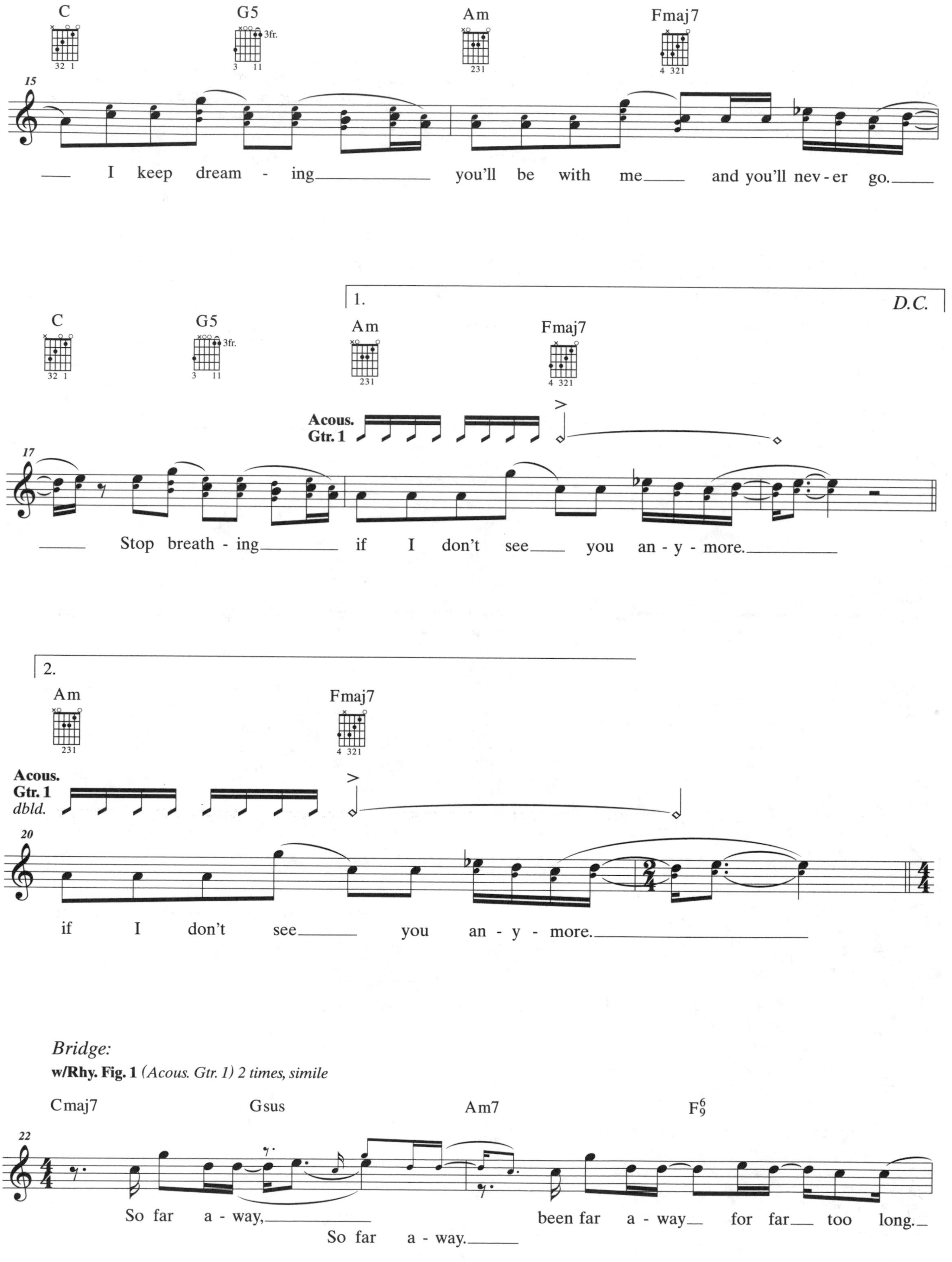
C
G5
3fr.
Am
Fmaj7
I keep dream - ing you'll be with me and you'll nev - er go.
1.
D.C.
Acous. Gtr. 1
Stop breath - ing if I don't see you an - y - more.
2.
Acous. Gtr. 1 dbld.
if I don't see you an - y - more.
Bridge:
w/Rhy. Fig. 1 (Acous. Gtr. 1) 2 times, simile
Cmaj7
Gsus
Am7
So far a - way, been far a - way for far too long.
So far a - way.

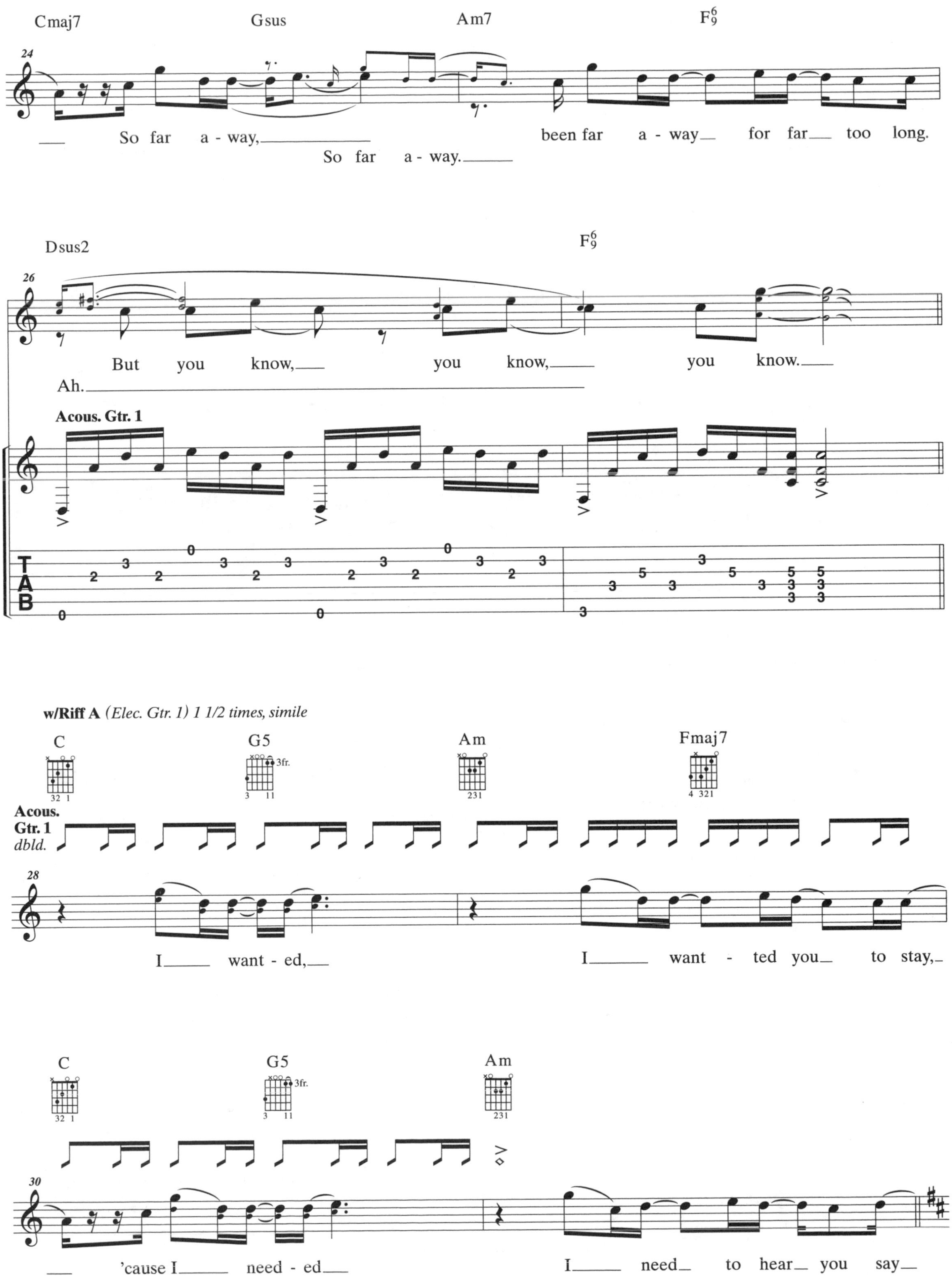
Cmaj7
Gsus
Am7
F6/9
So far a - way,
So far a - way.
been far a - way for far too long.
Dsus2
F6/9
But you know, you know, you know.
Ah.
Acous. Gtr. 1
T
A
B
w/Riff A (Elec. Gtr. 1) 1 1/2 times, simile
C
G5
Am
Fmaj7
Acous. Gtr. 1 dbld.
I want - ed,
I want - ted you to stay,
C
G5
Am
'cause I need - ed
I need to hear you say

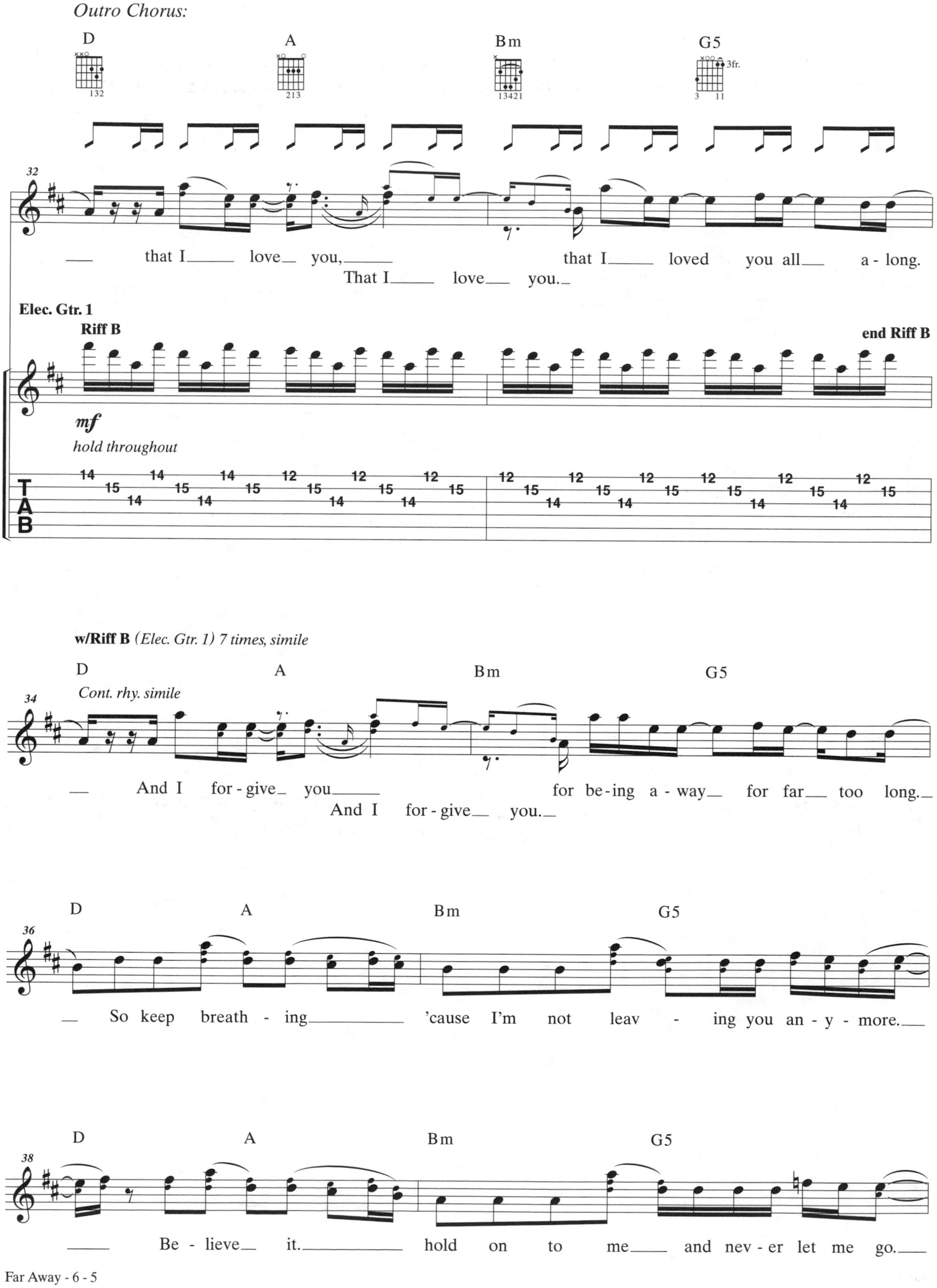
Outro Chorus:
D
A
Bm
G5
3fr.
32
— that I___ love_ you,_____ that I_____ loved you all___ a - long.
That I_____ love___ you._
Elec. Gtr. 1
Riff B
end Riff B
mf
hold throughout
w/Riff B (Elec. Gtr. 1) 7 times, simile
D
A
Bm
G5
34
Cont. rhy. simile
— And I for - give_ you_____ for be - ing a - way__ for far__ too long._
And I for - give__ you._
D
A
Bm
G5
36
— So keep breath - ing__________ 'cause I'm not leav - ing you an - y - more.___
D
A
Bm
G5
38
_____ Be - lieve_ it._________ hold on to me____ and nev - er let me go.___

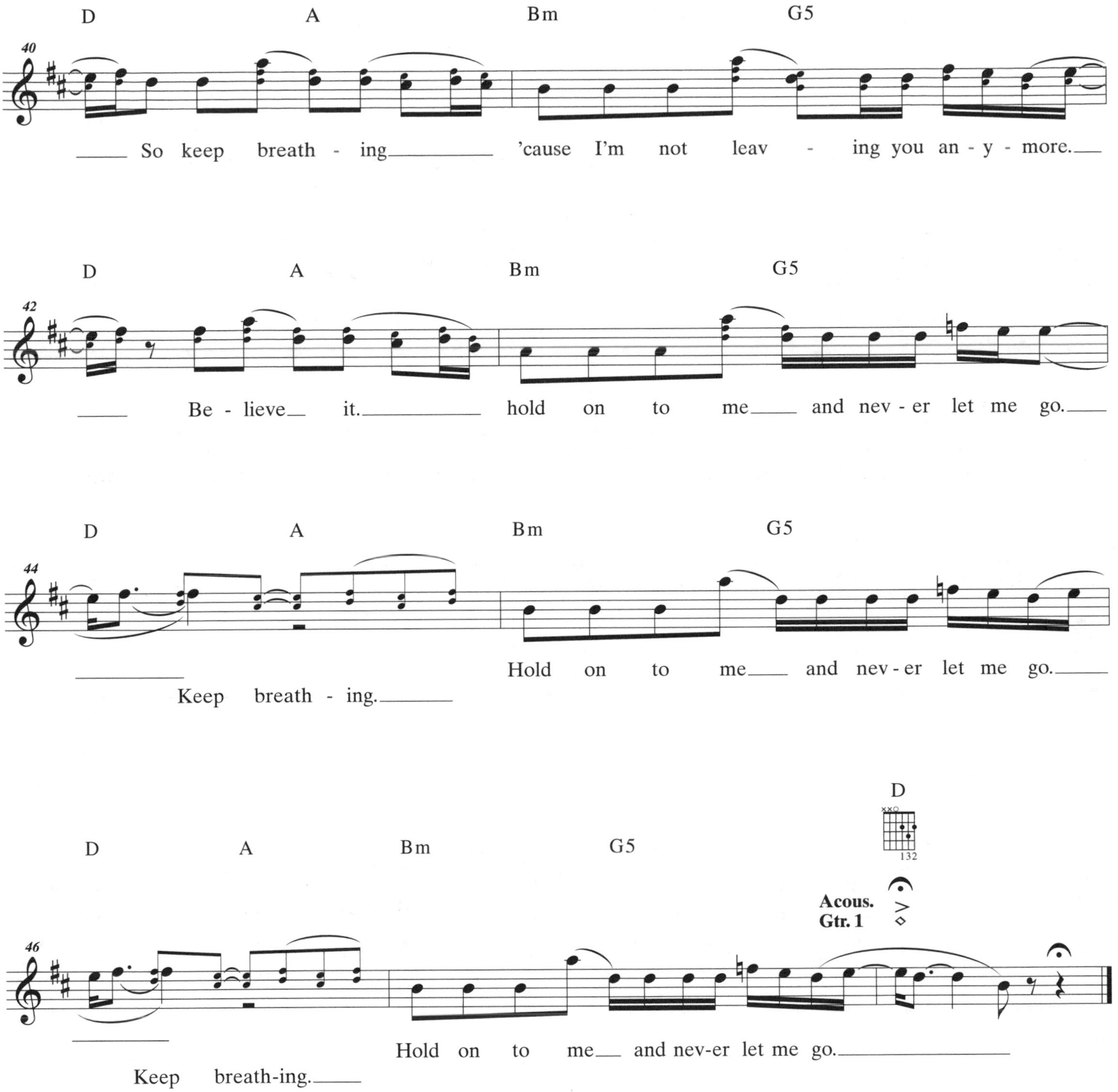
D A Bm G5
40
So keep breath - ing 'cause I'm not leav - ing you an - y - more.
D A Bm G5
42
Be - lieve it. hold on to me and nev - er let me go.
D A Bm G5
44
Hold on to me and nev - er let me go.
Keep breath - ing.
D A Bm G5 D
132
Acous. Gtr. 1
46
Hold on to me and nev-er let me go.
Keep breath-ing.

GOTTA BE SOMEBODY

Lyrics by CHAD KROEGER
Music by NICKELBACK

Band enters
F
C
3fr.
G
Am
Am/D
of, but dreams just aren't e - nough so I'll be wait - ing for the real thing,
2. To - night
I know it by the feel - ing.
out on the street out in the moon - light.
The mo - ment when we're
And damn it, this feels
meet - ing will play out like a scene straight off the sil - ver
too right. It's just like dé - jà vu, me stand - in' here with
screen. So I'll be hold - in' my breath right up to the end, un - til that mo - ment when
you. So I'll be hold - in' my breath. Could this be the end? Is it that mo - ment when

F
G
3fr.
Elec. Gtr. 1
— I find the one that I'll spend— for - ev - er with.—
— I find the one that I'll spend— for - ev - er with?—
'Cause
Cont. in slashes
Chorus:
C
Elec. Gtrs. 1 & 2
Cont. rhy. simile
no - bod - y wants— to be the last one there. 'Cause ev - 'ry - one wants— to feel like
Am
some - one cares. Some - one to love— with my life in their hands. There's
got - ta be some - bod - y for me like that. 'Cause no - bod - y wants— to go it
on their own. And ev - 'ry - one wants— to know they're not a - lone.
On their— own. Not a -

Am
F
42
Some-bod - y else___ that feels the same some - where. There's got - ta be some - bod - y for
lone. Same some - where.
1.
D.S. 𝄋
2.
45
me out there.________ me out there.________
Interlude:
Am
F
Elec. Gtrs. 1 & 2
47
Ah,________________________ ah ah ah ah ah ah,__________ ah ah ah
Am/D
F
51
ah ah ah,______________ ah ah ah ah ah ah ah ah ah. You
Bridge:
C
3fr.
G
3fr.
Elec. Gtrs. 1 & 2 resume chorus fig. simile
55
can't_____ give_____ up (when you're look - in' for) a dia - mond in the
Am
58
rough. (Be - cause you nev - er know,) when it_____ shows____ up, (make sure you're hold - in' on)

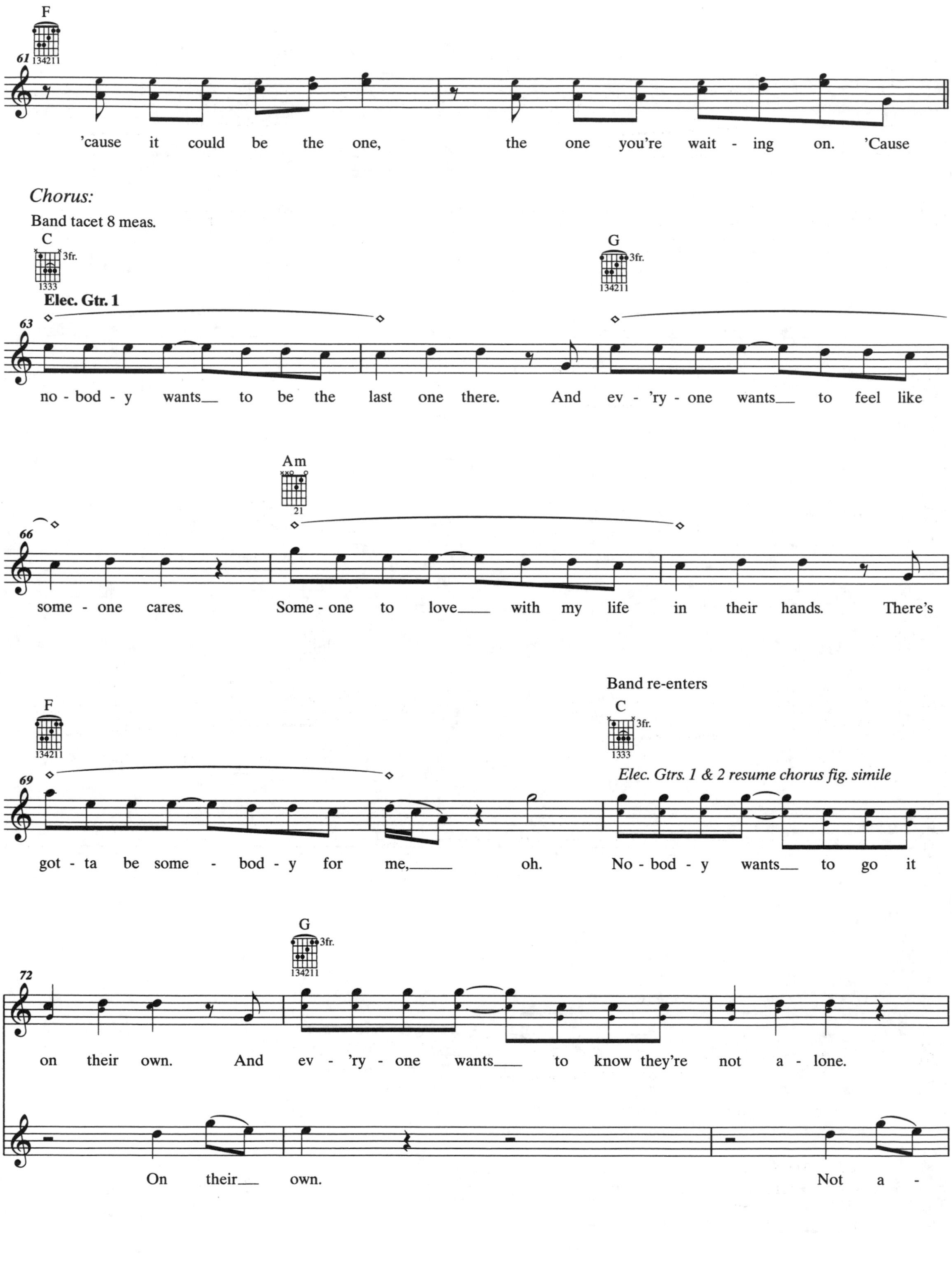
F
134211
61
'cause it could be the one, the one you're wait - ing on. 'Cause
Chorus:
Band tacet 8 meas.
C
3fr.
1333
Elec. Gtr. 1
63
G
3fr.
134211
no - bod - y wants__ to be the last one there. And ev - 'ry - one wants__ to feel like
Am
21
66
some - one cares. Some - one to love__ with my life in their hands. There's
F
134211
69
Band re-enters
C
3fr.
1333
Elec. Gtrs. 1 & 2 resume chorus fig. simile
got - ta be some - bod - y for me,__ oh. No - bod - y wants__ to go it
G
3fr.
134211
72
on their own. And ev - 'ry - one wants__ to know they're not a - lone.
On their__ own. Not a -

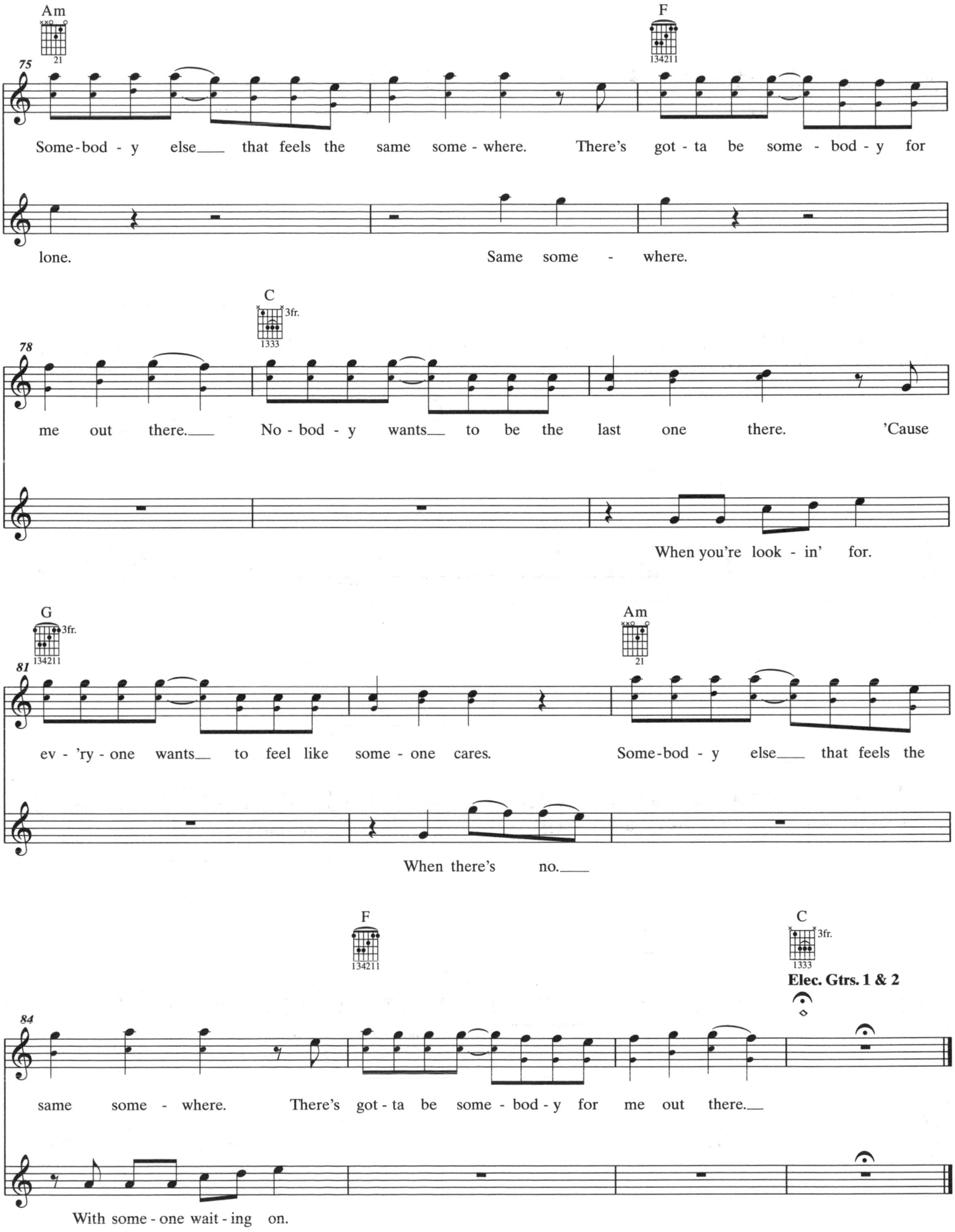
Am
F
75
Some-bod - y else___ that feels the same some - where. There's got - ta be some - bod - y for
lone. Same some - where.
C
78
me out there.___ No - bod - y wants__ to be the last one there. 'Cause
When you're look - in' for.
G
Am
81
ev - 'ry - one wants__ to feel like some - one cares. Some-bod - y else___ that feels the
When there's no.___
F
C
Elec. Gtrs. 1 & 2
84
same some - where. There's got - ta be some - bod - y for me out there.__
With some - one wait - ing on.

PHOTOGRAPH

*Tune down 1/2 step:
⑥ = E♭ ③ = G♭
⑤ = A♭ ② = B♭
④ = D♭ ① = E♭

Lyrics by CHAD KROEGER
Music by NICKELBACK

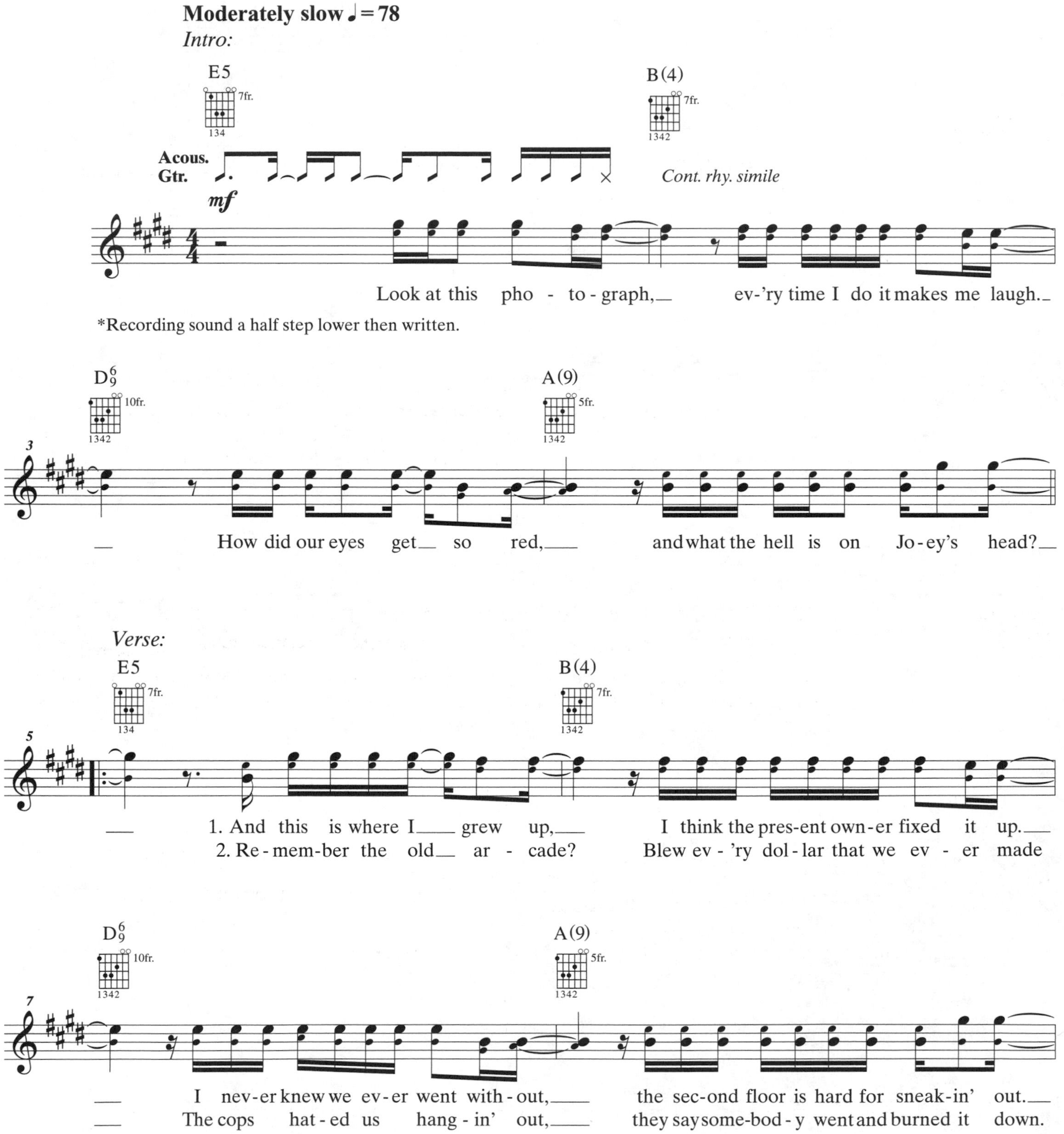
Moderately slow ♩ = 78
Intro:
E5
B(4)
Acous. Gtr.
mf
Cont. rhy. simile
Look at this pho - to - graph, ev-'ry time I do it makes me laugh.
*Recording sound a half step lower then written.
D6/9
A(9)
How did our eyes get so red, and what the hell is on Jo-ey's head?
Verse:
E5
B(4)
1. And this is where I grew up, I think the pres-ent own-er fixed it up.
2. Re-mem-ber the old ar - cade? Blew ev - 'ry dol-lar that we ev - er made
D6/9
A(9)
I nev-er knew we ev-er went with-out, the sec-ond floor is hard for sneak-in' out.
The cops hat-ed us hang-in' out, they say some-bod-y went and burned it down.

E5
7fr.
134
B(4)
7fr.
1342
And this is where I went to school, most of the time, had bet-ter things to do.
We used to lis-ten to the ra - di - o and sing a-long with ev-'ry song we'd know.
D6/9
10fr.
1342
Crim - i - nal rec - ord says I broke in twice,
We said some - day we'd find out how it feels
A(9)
5fr.
1342
I must have done it half a doz - en times.
to sing to more than just the steer - ing wheel.
E5
7fr.
134
B(4)
7fr.
1342
I won-der if it's too late, should I go back and try to grad - u - ate?
Kim's the first girl I kissed, I was so ner-vous that I near - ly missed.
D6/9
10fr.
1342
A(9)
5fr.
1342
Life's bet-ter now then it was back then, if I was them I would-n't let me in.
She's had a cou-ple of kids since then, I have-n't seen her since God knows when.
G6
3fr.
1342
A(9)
5fr.
1342
Oh, whoa whoa, oh, God I, I... Ev - 'ry

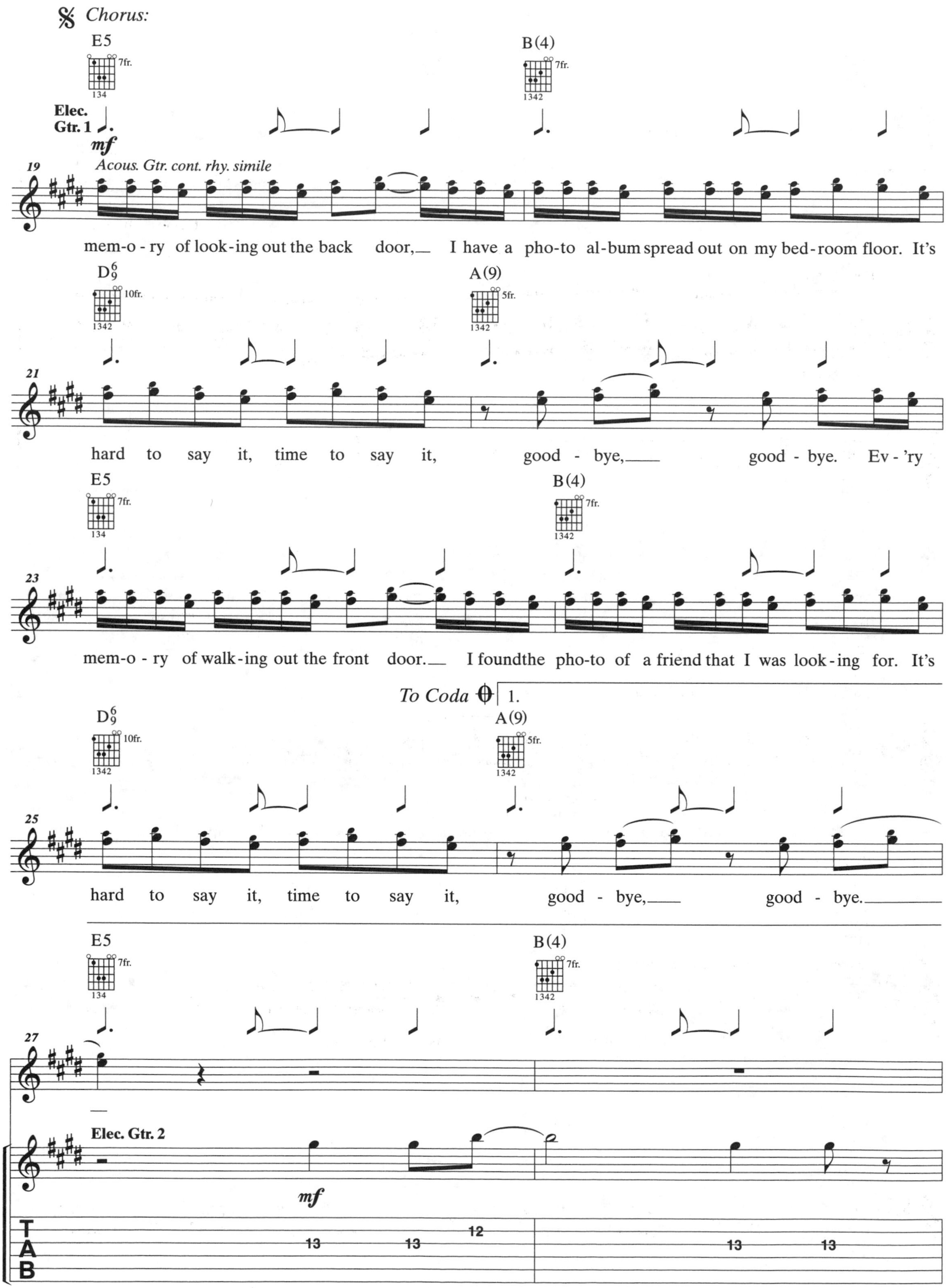
Chorus:
E5
B(4)
Elec. Gtr. 1
mf
Acous. Gtr. cont. rhy. simile
mem-o - ry of look-ing out the back door, I have a pho-to al-bum spread out on my bed-room floor. It's
D6/9
A(9)
hard to say it, time to say it, good - bye, good - bye. Ev - 'ry
E5
B(4)
mem-o - ry of walk-ing out the front door. I foundthe pho-to of a friend that I was look-ing for. It's
To Coda
1.
D6/9
A(9)
hard to say it, time to say it, good - bye, good - bye.
E5
B(4)
Elec. Gtr. 2
mf

G6
3fr.
1342
A(9)
5fr.
1342
29
Good - bye.
Elec. Gtr. 2
Elec. Gtr. 3
T
A
B
12 10 8 12 10 8 8 7 0 2 4
12 11 9 12 11 9 9 7 9
9
2.
A(9)
5fr.
1342
Cmaj7
8fr.
1342
10fr.
1342
31
Good - bye, good - bye.
Bridge:
E5
7fr.
134
B(4)
7fr.
1342
G6
3fr.
1342
34
Acous. Gtr. & Elec. Gtr. 1 cont. simile
I miss that town, I miss their fac - es. You can't e - rase,
A(9)
5fr.
1342
E5
7fr.
134
B(4)
7fr.
1342
37
you can't re - place it. I miss it now, I can't be - lieve

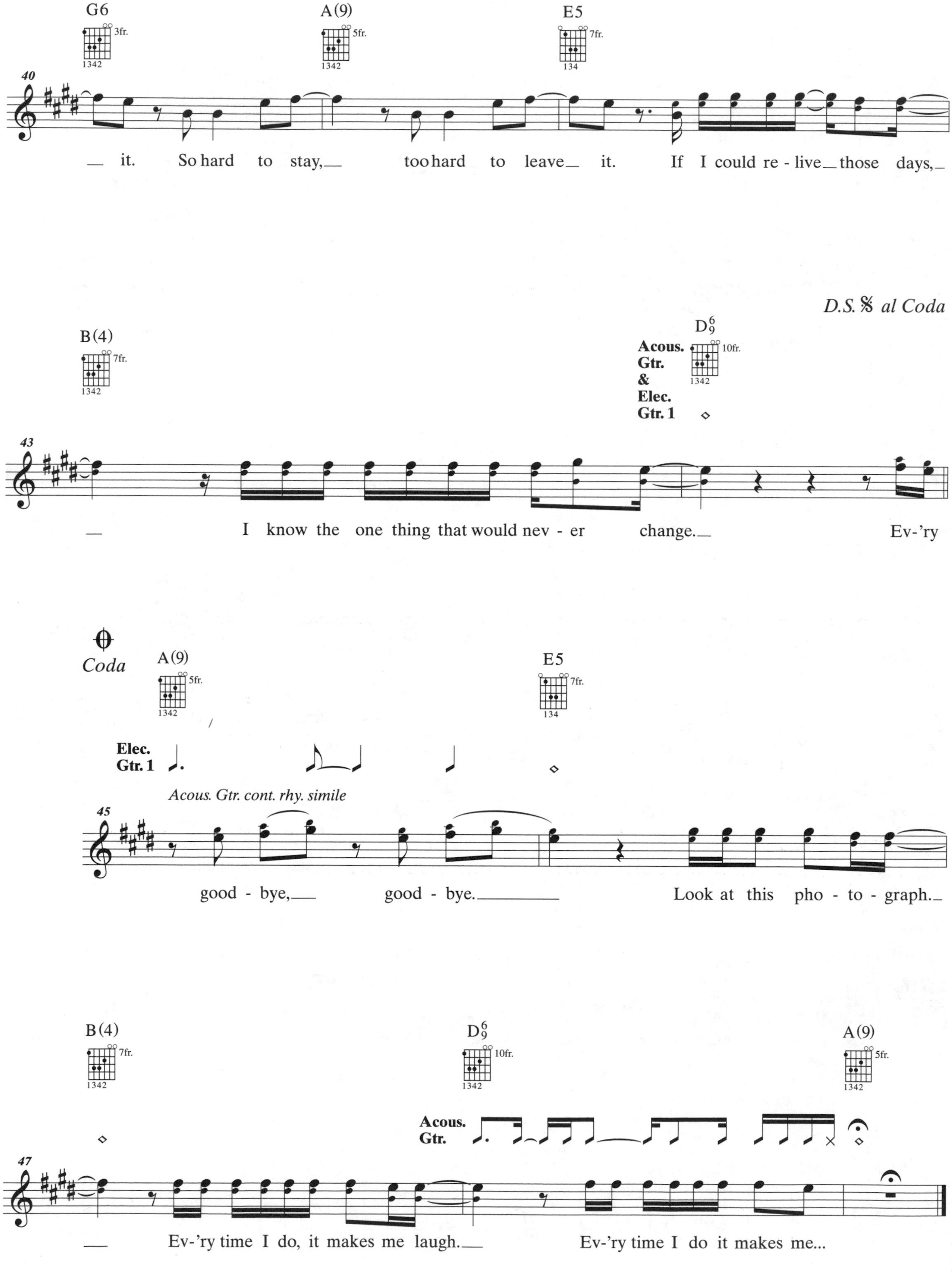
G6
A(9)
E5
40
it. So hard to stay, too hard to leave it. If I could re-live those days,
D.S. 𝄋 al Coda
B(4)
Acous. Gtr. & Elec. Gtr. 1
D6/9
43
I know the one thing that would nev-er change. Ev-'ry
Coda
A(9)
E5
Elec. Gtr. 1
Acous. Gtr. cont. rhy. simile
45
good-bye, good-bye. Look at this pho-to-graph.
B(4)
D6/9
A(9)
Acous. Gtr.
47
Ev-'ry time I do, it makes me laugh. Ev-'ry time I do it makes me...

ROCKSTAR

Lyrics by CHAD KROEGER
Music by NICKELBACK

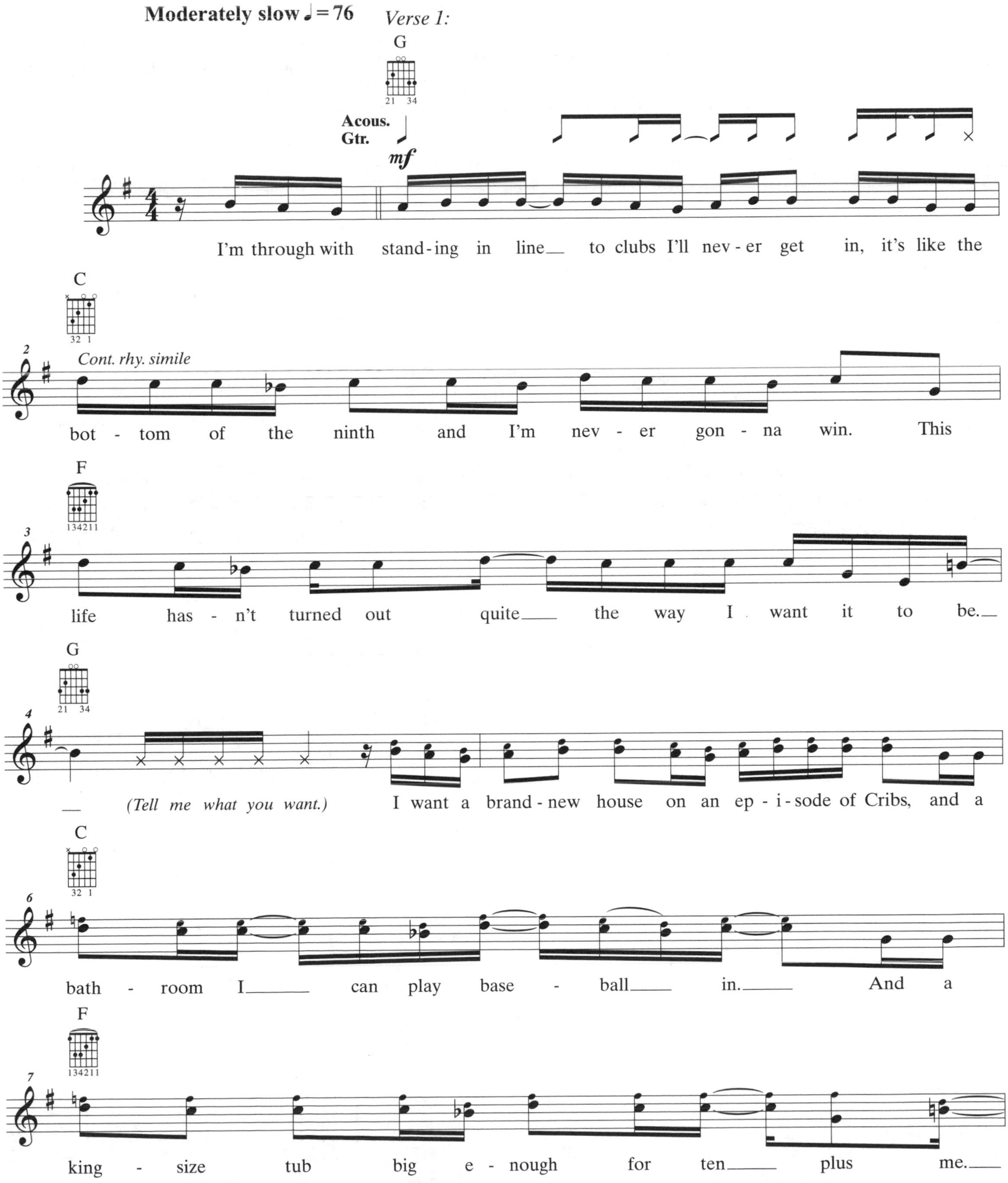
Moderately slow ♩ = 76
Verse 1:
G
Acous. Gtr.
mf
I'm through with stand-ing in line__ to clubs I'll nev-er get in, it's like the
C
Cont. rhy. simile
bot - tom of the ninth and I'm nev - er gon - na win. This
F
life has - n't turned out quite__ the way I want it to be.__
G
__ (Tell me what you want.) I want a brand-new house on an ep - i - sode of Cribs, and a
C
bath - room I__ can play base - ball__ in.__ And a
F
king - size tub big e - nough for ten__ plus me.__

Verses 2 & 3:
G
C
F
Elec. Gtr. 1
mf
— (Go for what you need.) 2. I'll need a, a cred-it card that's got no lim - it and a
3. See additional lyrics
big black jet with a bath - room in it. Gon-na join the mile high club at thir-ty-sev-en thou-sand feet.
— (Been there, done that.) I want a new tour bus full of old gui - tars, my own
star on Hol-ly-wood Bou - le - vard. Some-where be-tween Cher and James Dean is fine for me.

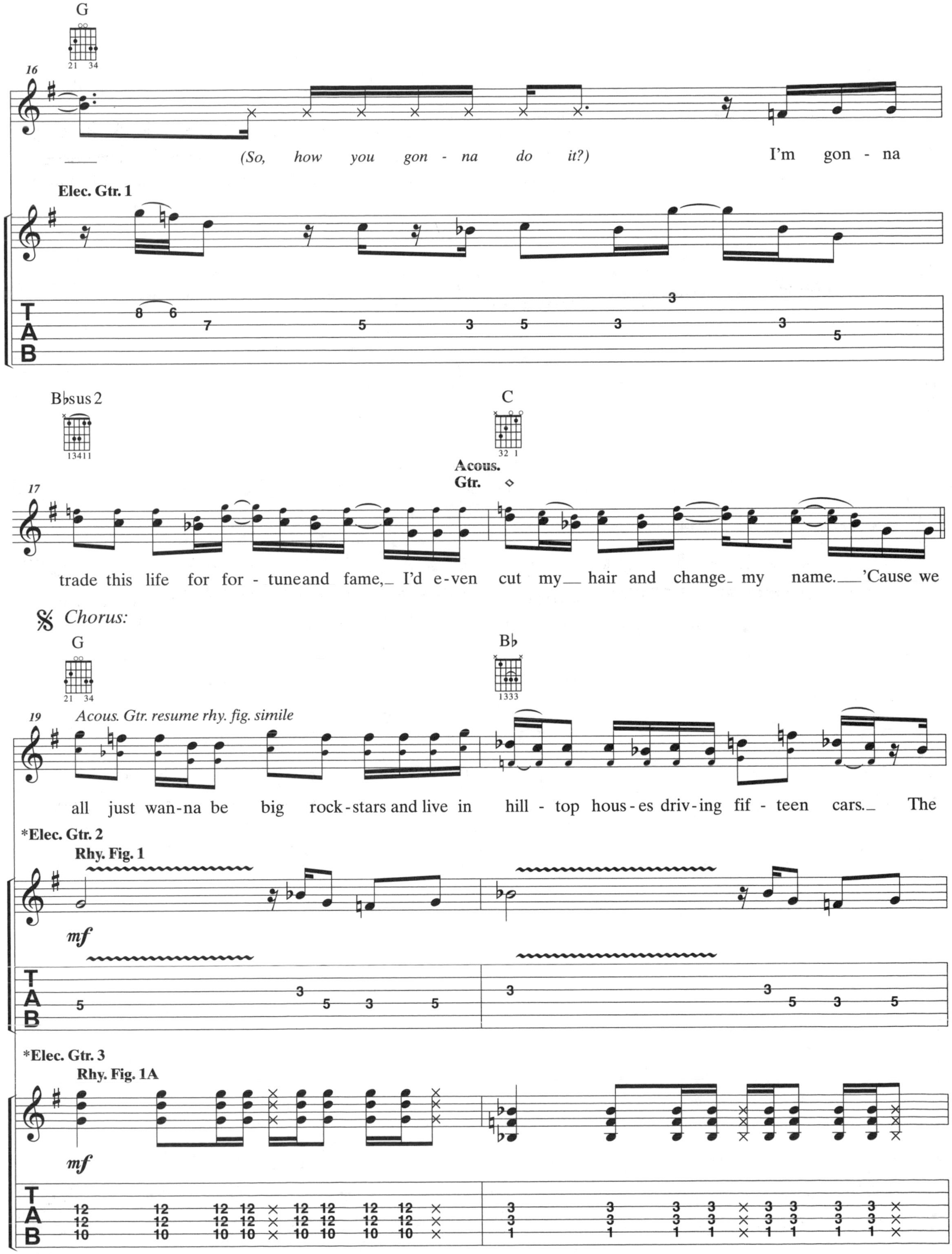
G
16
(So, how you gon - na do it?) I'm gon - na
Elec. Gtr. 1
T A B
B♭sus2
C
Acous. Gtr.
17
trade this life for for - tune and fame, I'd e-ven cut my hair and change my name. 'Cause we
𝄋 Chorus:
G
B♭
19
Acous. Gtr. resume rhy. fig. simile
all just wan-na be big rock-stars and live in hill - top hous-es driv-ing fif - teen cars. The
*Elec. Gtr. 2
Rhy. Fig. 1
mf
*Elec. Gtr. 3
Rhy. Fig. 1A
mf

*Elec. Gtrs. 2 & 3 tacet 1st 4 meas., 3rd time only.

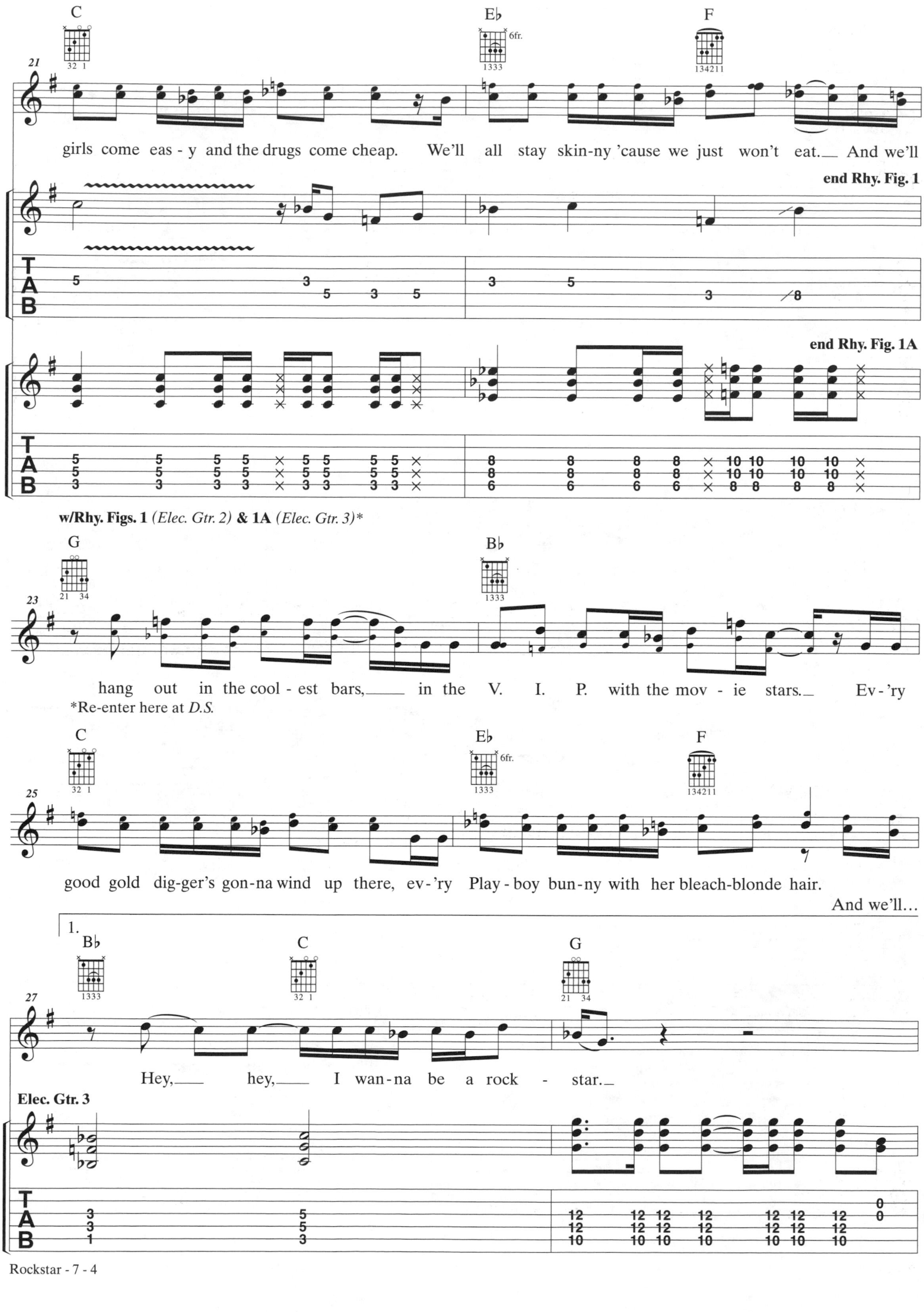
C
Eb
F
girls come eas - y and the drugs come cheap. We'll all stay skin-ny 'cause we just won't eat. And we'll
end Rhy. Fig. 1
end Rhy. Fig. 1A
w/Rhy. Figs. 1 (Elec. Gtr. 2) & 1A (Elec. Gtr. 3)*
G
Bb
hang out in the cool - est bars, in the V. I. P. with the mov - ie stars. Ev-'ry
*Re-enter here at D.S.
C
Eb
F
good gold dig-ger's gon-na wind up there, ev-'ry Play-boy bun-ny with her bleach-blonde hair.
And we'll...
1.
Bb
C
G
Hey, hey, I wan-na be a rock - star.
Elec. Gtr. 3

Bbsus2
C
G
Acous. Gtr.
29
Hey, hey, I wan-na be a rock - star.
3. I wan-na be
T
A
B
2. 3.
w/Rhy. Figs. 1 (Elec. Gtr. 2) & 1A (Elec. Gtr. 3)
G
31
hide out in the pri - vate rooms with the
B♭
32
lat - est dic - tion - ar - y and to - day's who's who. They'll
C
33
get you an - y - thing with that e - vil smile. Ev - 'ry -
E♭
6fr.
F
To Coda
34
bod - y's got a drug deal - er on speed di - al.

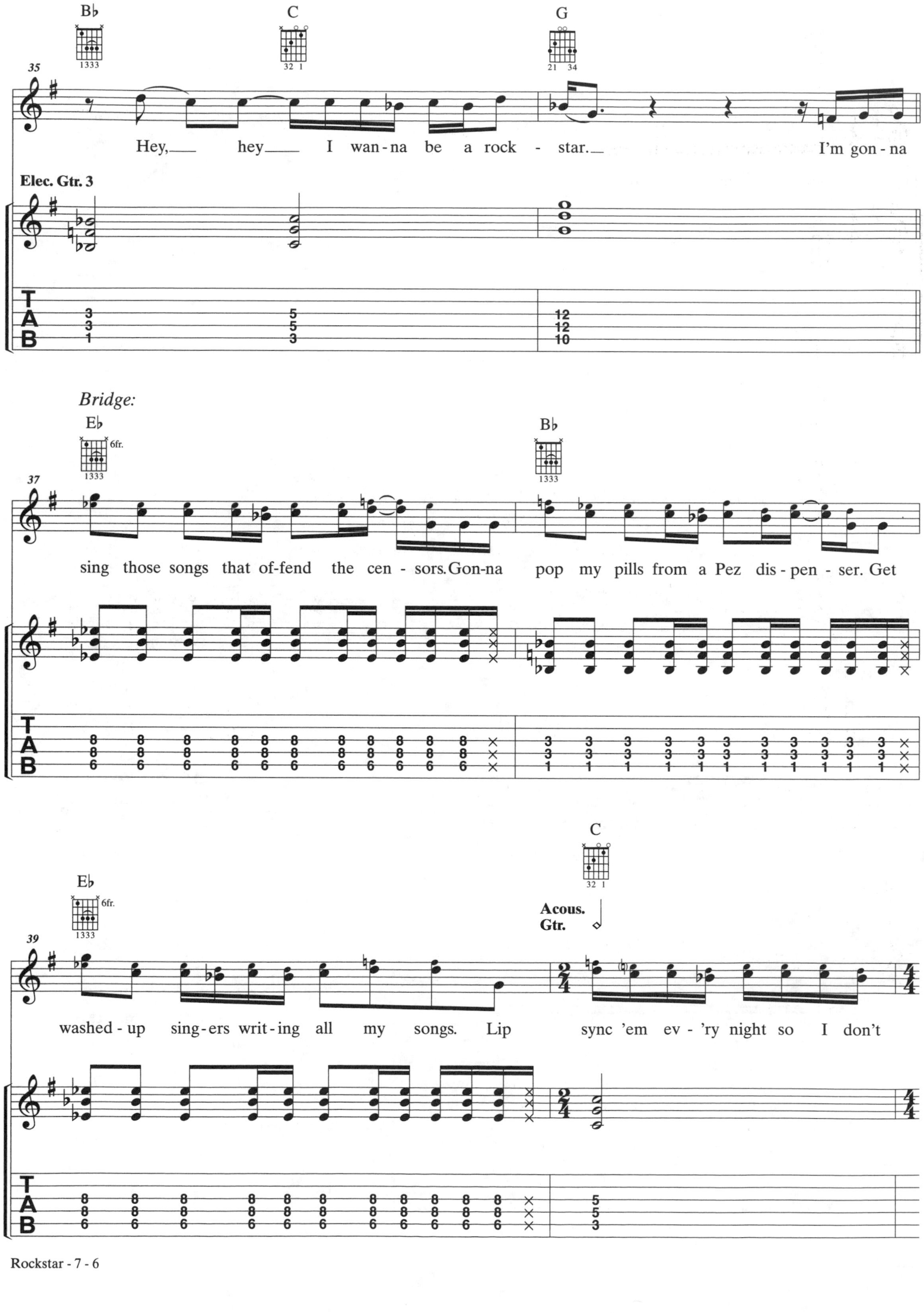
B♭
C
G
Hey, hey I wan-na be a rock - star. I'm gon-na
Elec. Gtr. 3
Bridge:
E♭
B♭
sing those songs that of-fend the cen - sors. Gon-na pop my pills from a Pez dis - pen - ser. Get
E♭
C
Acous. Gtr.
washed - up sing-ers writ-ing all my songs. Lip sync 'em ev - 'ry night so I don't

D.S. 𝄋 al Coda
F
get 'em wrong.
Well, we
Coda
B♭
C
G
Hey, hey, I wan-na be a rock - star.
Elec. Gtr. 3
Elec. Gtrs. tacet
B♭sus2
C
G
Acous. Gtr.
Hey, hey, I wan - na be a rock - star.

Verse 3:
I wanna be great like Elvis, without the tassels,
Hire eight bodyguards who love to beat up assholes.
Sign a couple autographs so I can eat my meals for free. *(I'll have the quesadilla, ha, ha.)*
I'm gonna dress my ass with the latest fashion,
Get a front door key to the Playboy mansion.
Gonna date a centerfold that loves to blow my money for me. *(So how ya gonna do it?)*
I'm gonna trade this life for fortune and fame,
I'd even cut my hair and change my name.
(To Chorus:)

CRUSHCRUSHCRUSH

*All Gtrs. in Drop D tuning, down 1/2 step:
⑥ = D♭ ③ = G♭
⑤ = A♭ ② = B♭
④ = D♭ ① = E♭

Words and Music by
HAYLEY WILLIAMS
and JOSH FARRO

*Recording sounds a half step lower than written.

Csus2
Dm
18
scrib-bled out the truth with their lies. Your lit-tle spies.
B♭5
A5
Elec. Gtr. 1
Elec. Gtr. 3 (w/dist.)
21
mf
T
A
B
Pre-chorus:
D5
Elec. Gtr. 1 dbld.
f
23
(Whispered) Crush, crush, crush, crush, crush.
Two, three, four!
Chorus:
D5
F5
Csus2
B♭5
D5
Csus2
Rhy. Fig. 1
27
Noth-ing com-pares to a qui-et eve-ning a-lone. Just the one, two
D5
F5
Csus2
30
of us who's count-ing on. That nev-er hap-pens. I guess I'm dream-ing a-gain.

B♭5
1.
C5
end Rhy. Fig. 1
Let's be more than this.
Interlude:
D5 C5 D5 C5 A/C♯
Elec. Gtr. 2 dbld. 8va
mf
2. If
Elec. Gtr. 1 dbld.
2.
Bridge:
C5 D5 F5 C5 B♭5 D5 F5 C5 B♭5
this now!
Elec. Gtr. 1
Rhy. Fig. 2
end Rhy. Fig. 2

w/Rhy. Fig. 2 (Elec. Gtr. 1) 3 times, simile
D5 F5 C5 B♭5 D5 F5 C5 B♭5
Rock and roll, ba-by. Don't you know that we're all a - lone_ now? I need some-thing to sing a - bout._
D5 F5 C5 B♭5
Rock and roll, hon - ey. Don't you know, ba - by,
Bkgd. Vcl.: Hey!
Riff A
end Riff A
Elec. Gtr. 3
mf
w/Riff A (Elec. Gtr. 3) 3 times, simile
D5 F5 C5 B♭5 D5 F5 C5
we're all a - lone?_ now? I need some-thing to sing a - bout._ Rock and roll, hon-ey.
Hey!
B♭5 D5 F5 C5 B♭5
Don't you know, ba - by, we're all a - lone_ now? Give me some thing to sing a - bout._
Outro Chorus:
w/Rhy. Fig. 1 (Elec. Gtr. 1) simile on repeat
D5 F5 C5 B♭5 D5 C5
Elec. Gtr. 1 dbld.
Noth - ing_ com - pares_ to_ a qui - et eve-ning a - lone._ Just_ the_ one, two_

A/C♯ D5 F5 Csus2
of us who's count-ing on. That nev - er hap - pens. I guess I'm dream-ing a - gain.
B♭5
1. C5
2. C5
Let's be more than no, oh! more than this.
D5 A/C♯ C5 G/B
Oh, ho. Mm.
Elec. Gtr. 3
mf w/octave effect
A5 C5 A/C♯ D5

HALLELUJAH

All Gtrs. in Drop D tuning: ⑥ = D

Words and Music by
HAYLEY WILLIAMS
and JOSH FARRO

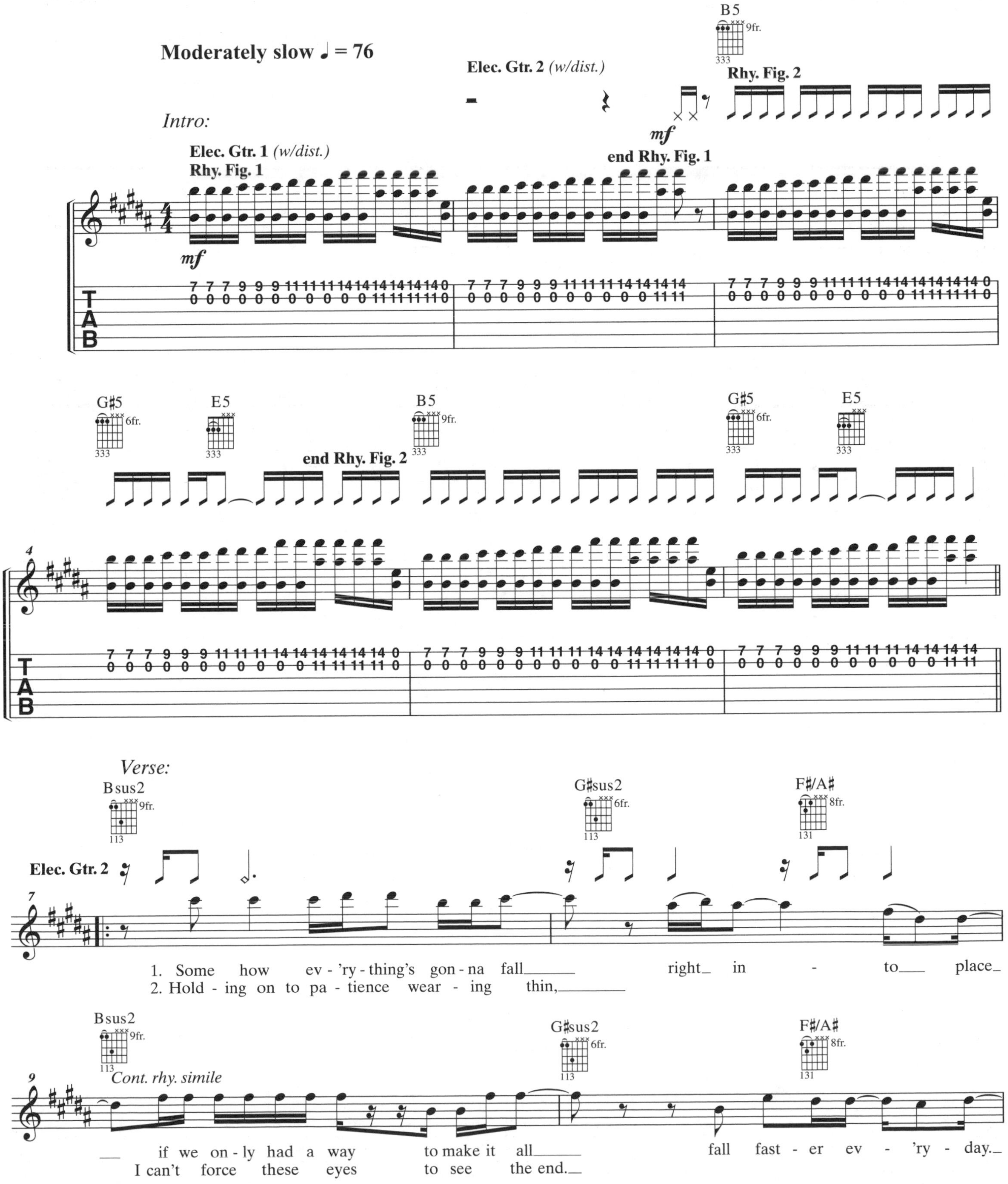

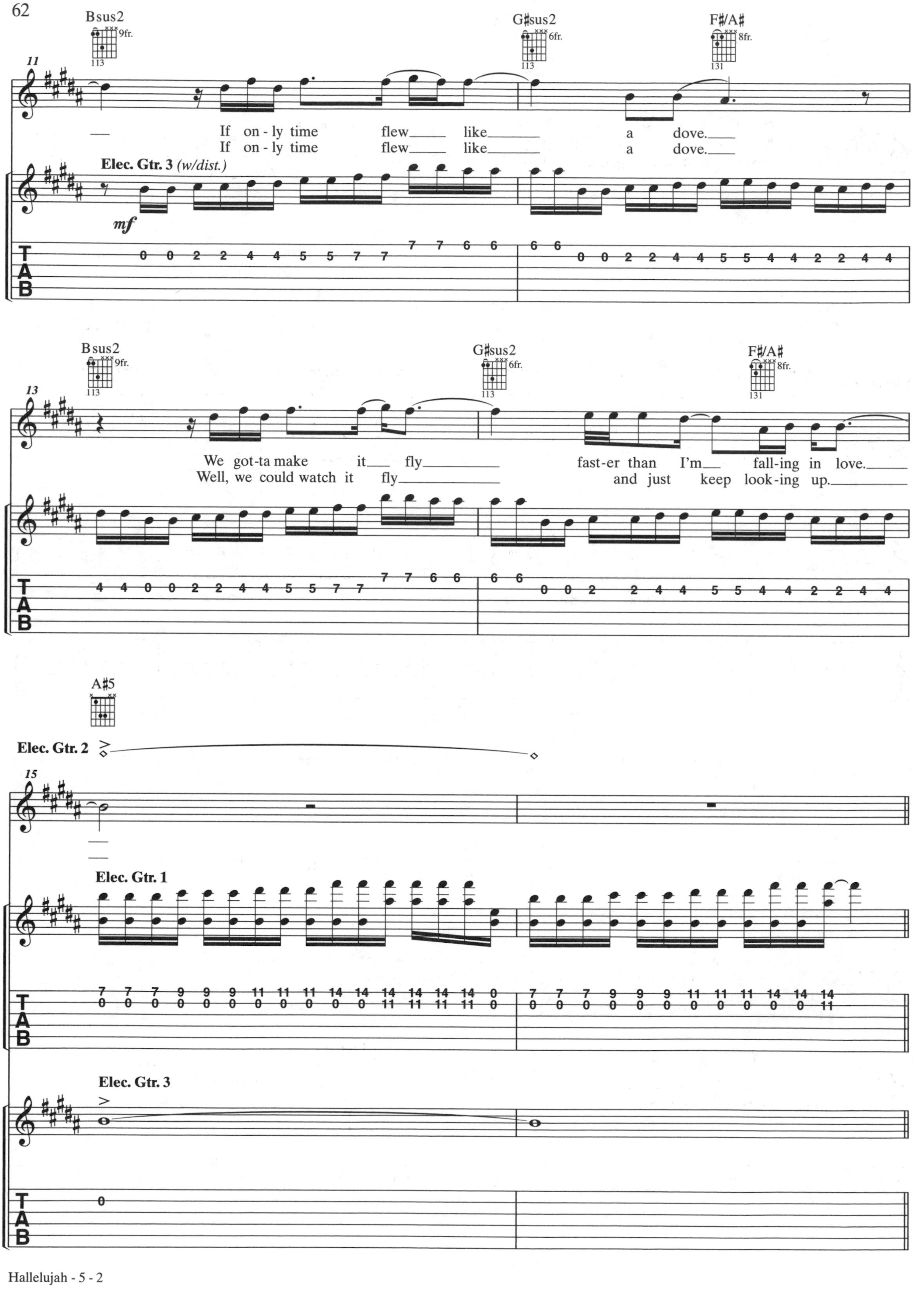
Bsus2
G♯sus2
F♯/A♯
If on-ly time flew like a dove.
If on-ly time flew like a dove.
Elec. Gtr. 3 (w/dist.)
mf
We got-ta make it fly faster than I'm fall-ing in love.
Well, we could watch it fly and just keep look-ing up.
A♯5
Elec. Gtr. 2
Elec. Gtr. 1
Elec. Gtr. 3

Chorus:

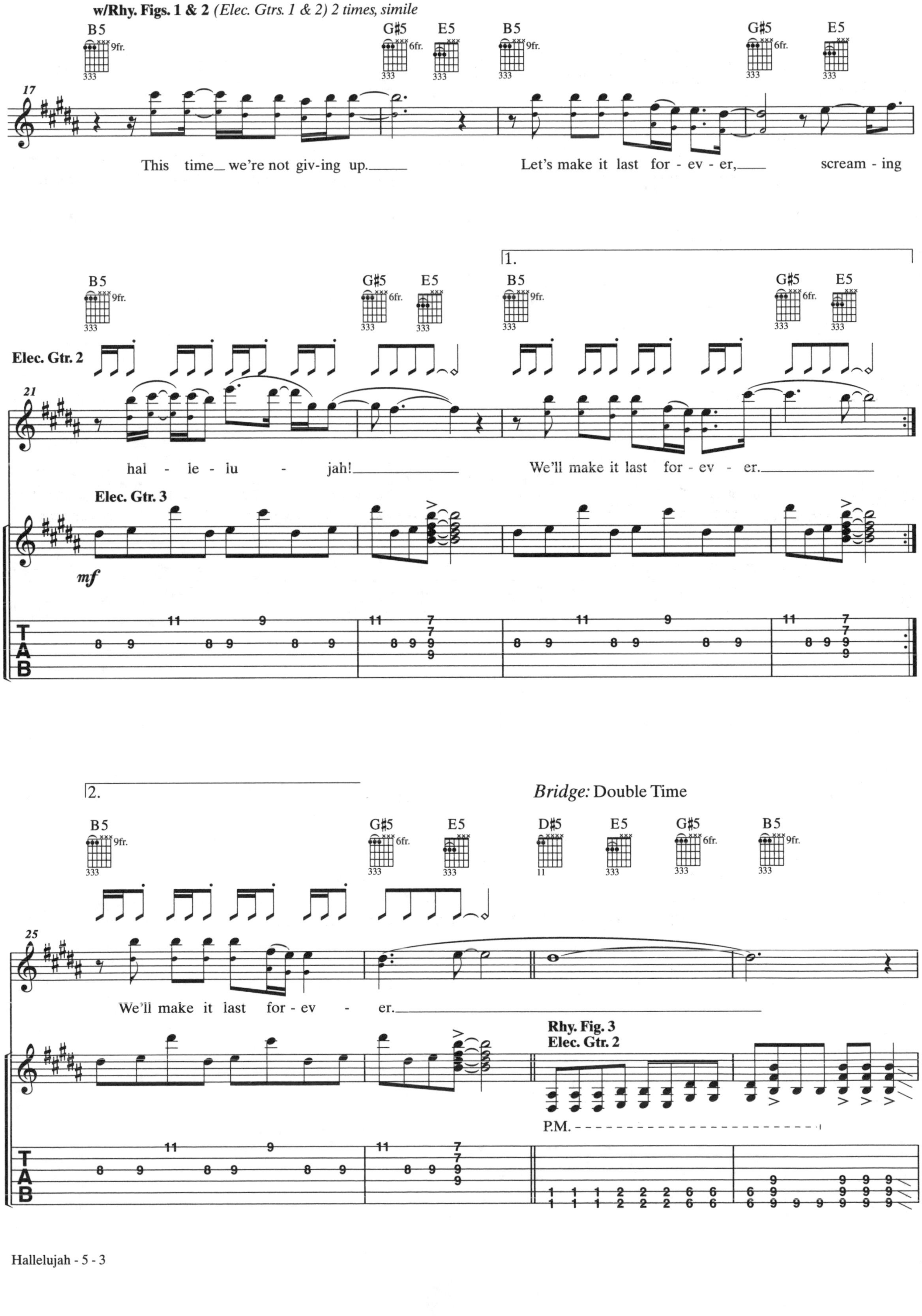
w/Rhy. Figs. 1 & 2 (Elec. Gtrs. 1 & 2) 2 times, simile
B5 G♯5 E5 B5 G♯5 E5
This time_ we're not giv-ing up.
Let's make it last for - ev - er,
scream - ing
1.
Elec. Gtr. 2
hal - le - lu - jah!
We'll make it last for - ev - er.
Elec. Gtr. 3
mf
2.
Bridge: Double Time
D♯5 E5 G♯5 B5
We'll make it last for - ev - er.
Rhy. Fig. 3
Elec. Gtr. 2
P.M.

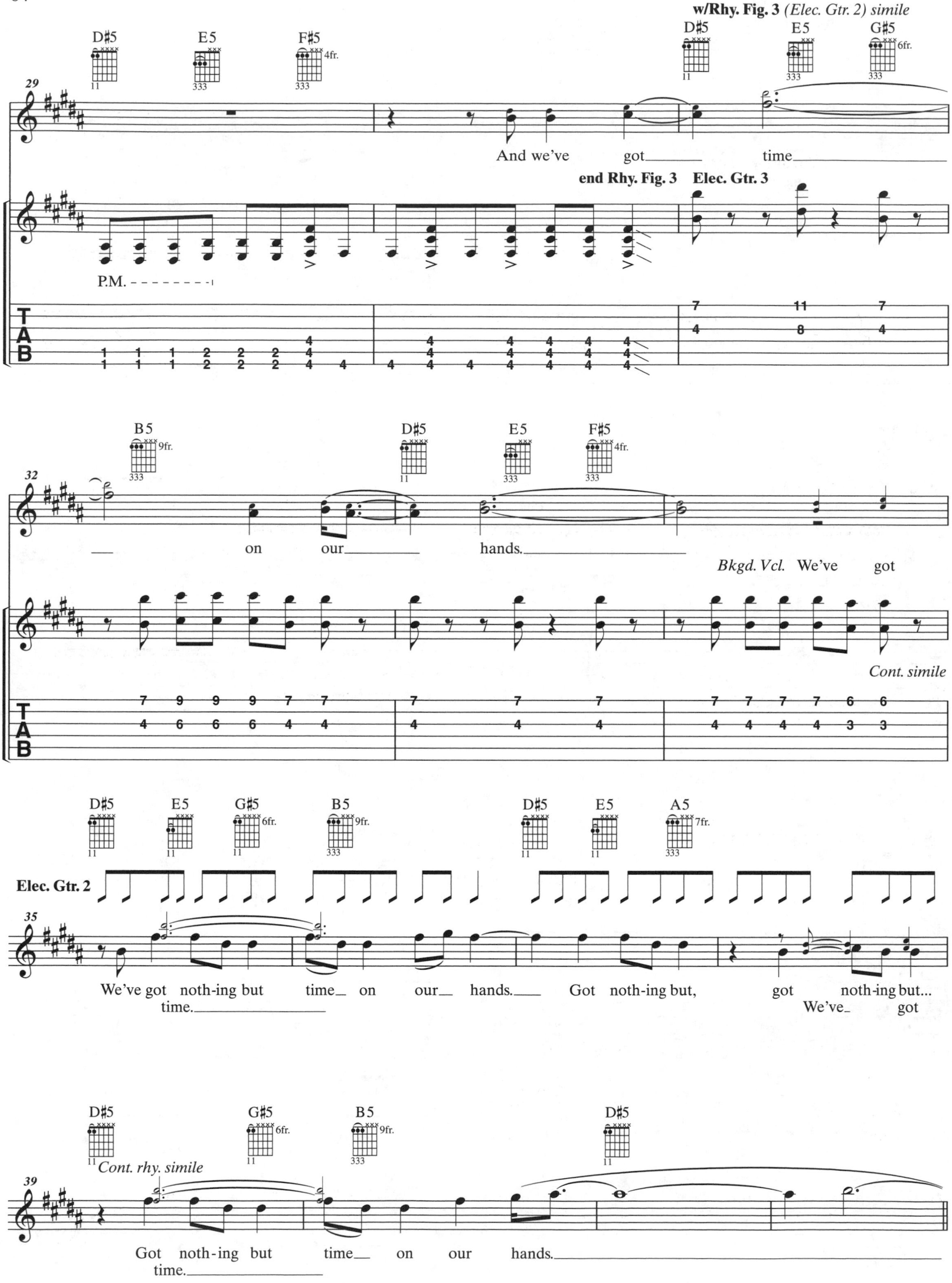
w/Rhy. Fig. 3 (Elec. Gtr. 2) simile
D♯5 E5 F♯5 D♯5 E5 G♯5
And we've got time
end Rhy. Fig. 3 Elec. Gtr. 3
P.M.
B5 D♯5 E5 F♯5
on our hands.
Bkgd. Vcl. We've got
Cont. simile
D♯5 E5 G♯5 B5 D♯5 E5 A5
Elec. Gtr. 2
We've got noth-ing but time on our hands. Got noth-ing but, got noth-ing but...
time. We've got
D♯5 G♯5 B5 D♯5
Cont. rhy. simile
Got noth-ing but time on our hands.
time.

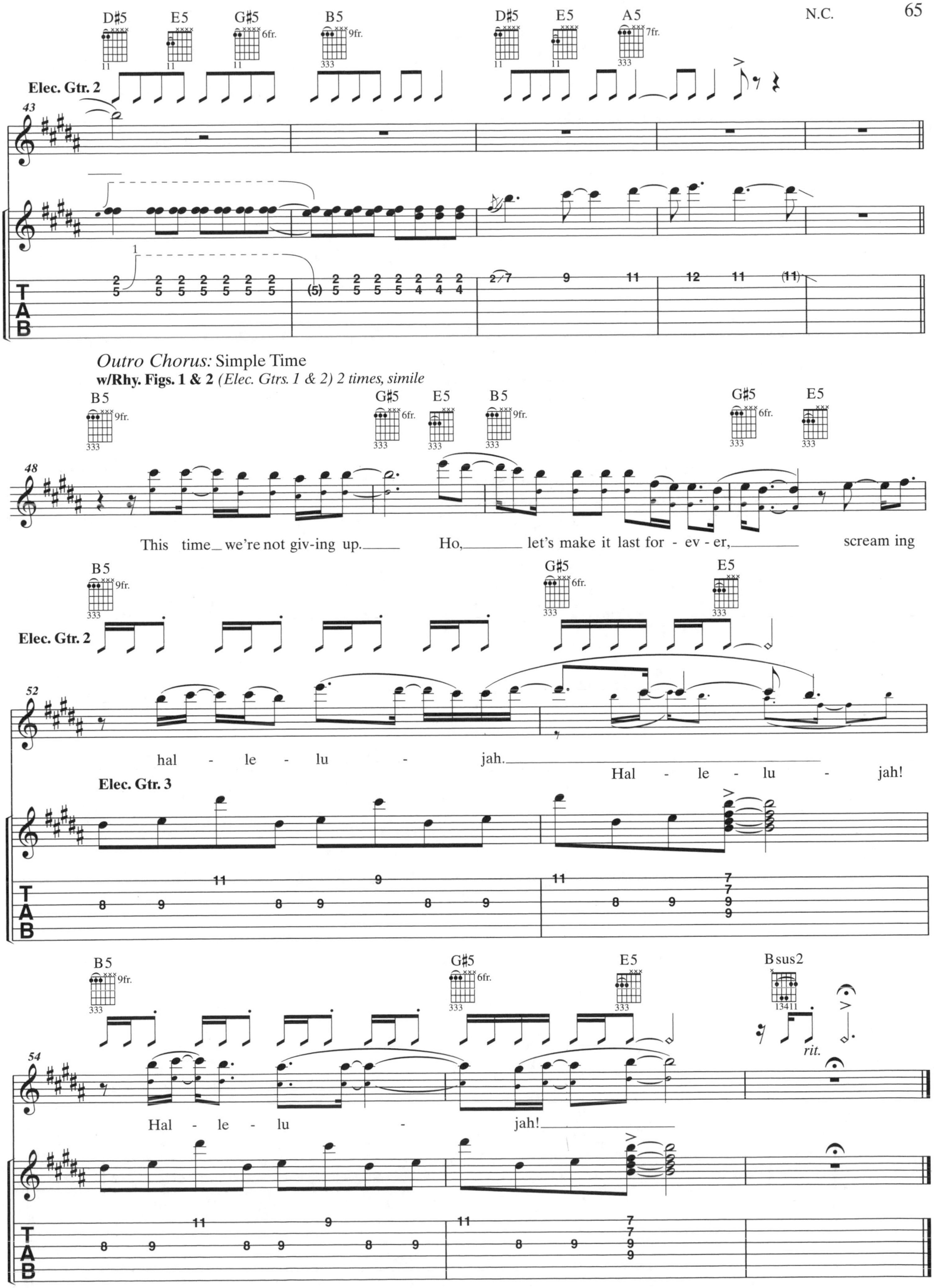
D♯5 E5 G♯5 B5 D♯5 E5 A5 N.C.
Elec. Gtr. 2
Outro Chorus: Simple Time
w/Rhy. Figs. 1 & 2 (Elec. Gtrs. 1 & 2) 2 times, simile
B5 G♯5 E5 B5 G♯5 E5
This time we're not giv-ing up. Ho, let's make it last for - ev - er, scream ing
B5 G♯5 E5
Elec. Gtr. 2
hal - le - lu - jah.
Hal - le - lu - jah!
Elec. Gtr. 3
B5 G♯5 E5 Bsus2
rit.
Hal - le - lu - jah!

MISERY BUSINESS

*All Gtrs. in Drop D tuning, down 1/2 step:
⑥ = D♭ ③ = G♭
⑤ = A♭ ② = B♭
④ = D♭ ① = E♭

Words and Music by
HAYLEY WILLIAMS
and JOSH FARRO

Moderately fast ♩ = 170
Intro:

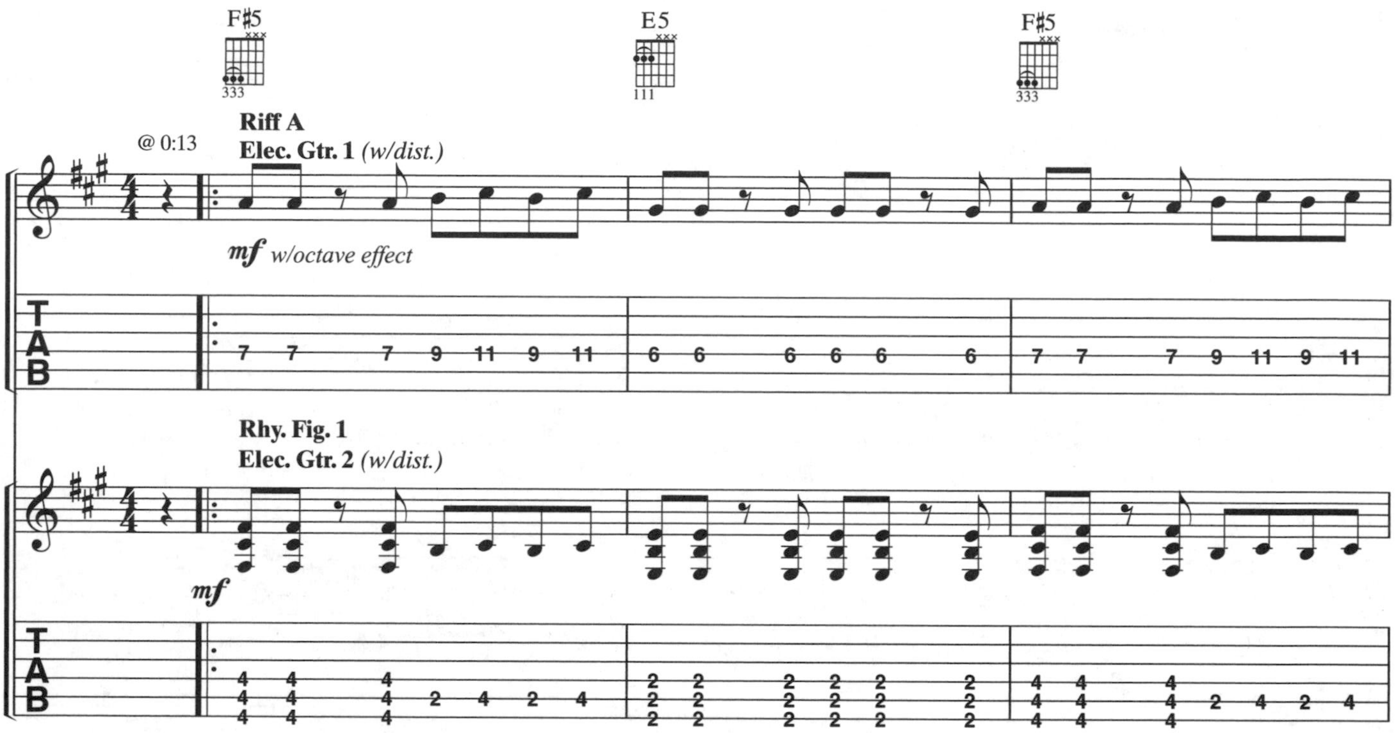

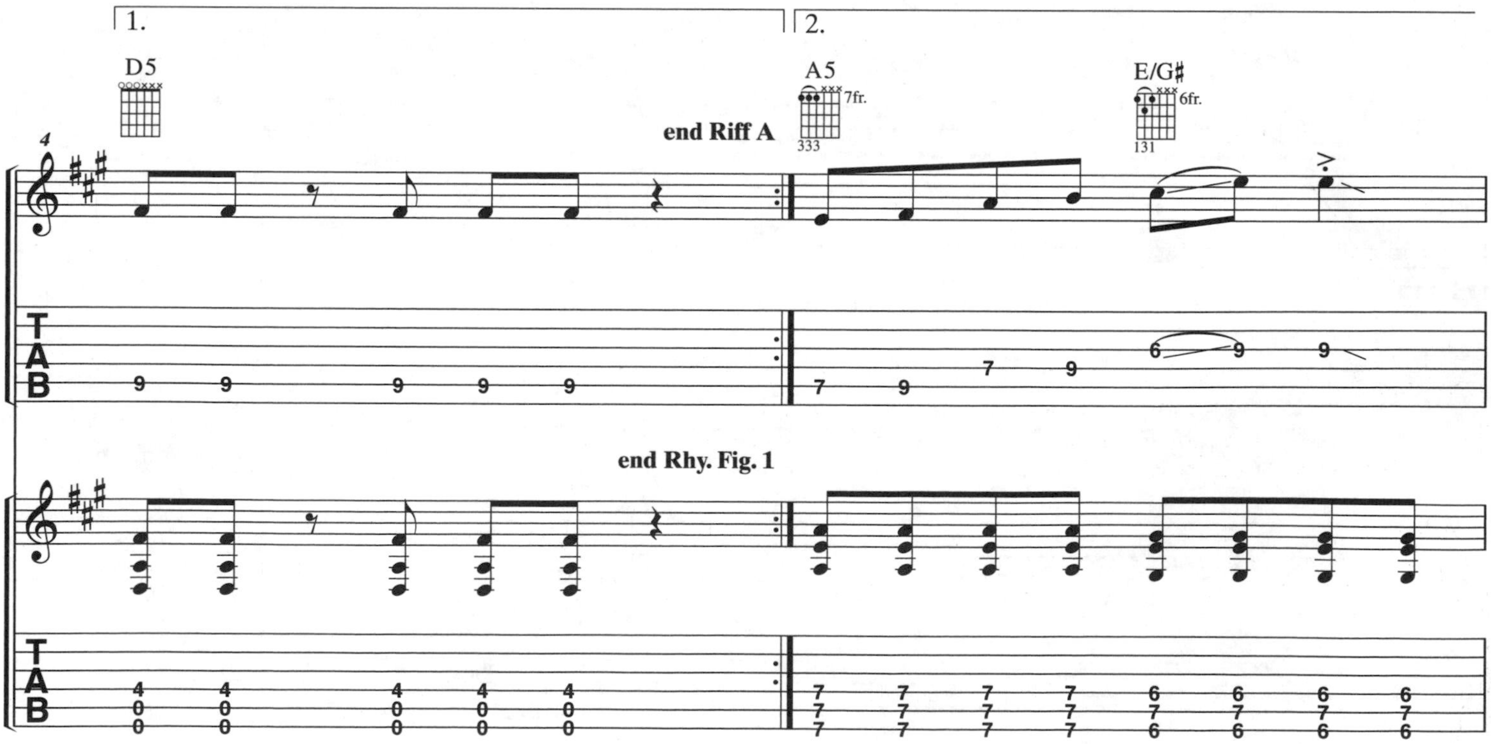

*Recording sounds a half step lower than written.

F♯5
E5
F♯5
1. I'm in the bus-'ness of mis - er - y, let's take it from the top. She's got a bod - y like an
2. Sec-ond chanc-es, they don't nev-er mat-ter, peo-ple nev-er change.__ Once a whore, you're noth-ing
Rhy. Fig. 2
Elec. Gtr. 2
P.M. throughout
D5
F♯5
E5
hour - glass, it's tick-ing like a clock. It's a mat-ter of time__ be-fore we all run out._
more. I'm sor - ry that -'ll nev - er change. And a bout for-give - ness,__ we're both sup-posed to have ex -
w/Rhy. Fig. 2 (Elec. Gtr. 2) simile
F♯5
A5
E/G♯
F♯5
__ When I thought he was mine,__ she caught him by the mouth. I wait-ed eight long months,_
changed. Sor - ry, hon - ey, but I passed up, now look this way! Well, give us a mil - lion oth - er
end Rhy. Fig. 2
Elec. Gtr. 1
P.M. throughout

E5
F♯5
D5
15
— she fi - n'lly set him free.— I told him I could - n't lie, — he was the on - ly one for
girls who do it just like you.— Look - ing as in - no - cent as pos - si - ble to get to who.
F♯5
E5
F♯5
18
me. Two weeks, we caught on fire.— She's got it out for— me,— but I wear the
They want it, what they like, it's eas - y if you do it right.— Well, I re - fuse, I re -
A5
7fr.
E/G♯
6fr.
F♯m
E
21
Acous. Gtr.
big - gest smile.—
fuse, I re - fuse!—
Elec. Gtrs. 1 & 2
Elec. Gtr. 2 cont. in slashes

Chorus:
D
A
E5
F♯m
F♯sus2
Elec. Gtr. 2
Cont. rhy. simile
Whoa, I nev - er meant to brag, but I got him where I want him now.
Elec. Gtr. 1
mp
Whoa, it was nev-er my in-ten tion to brag, to steal it all a - way from you now.
D5
F♯5
E5
F♯5
But, God, does it feel so good, 'cause I got him where I want him now.

* Composite arrangement.

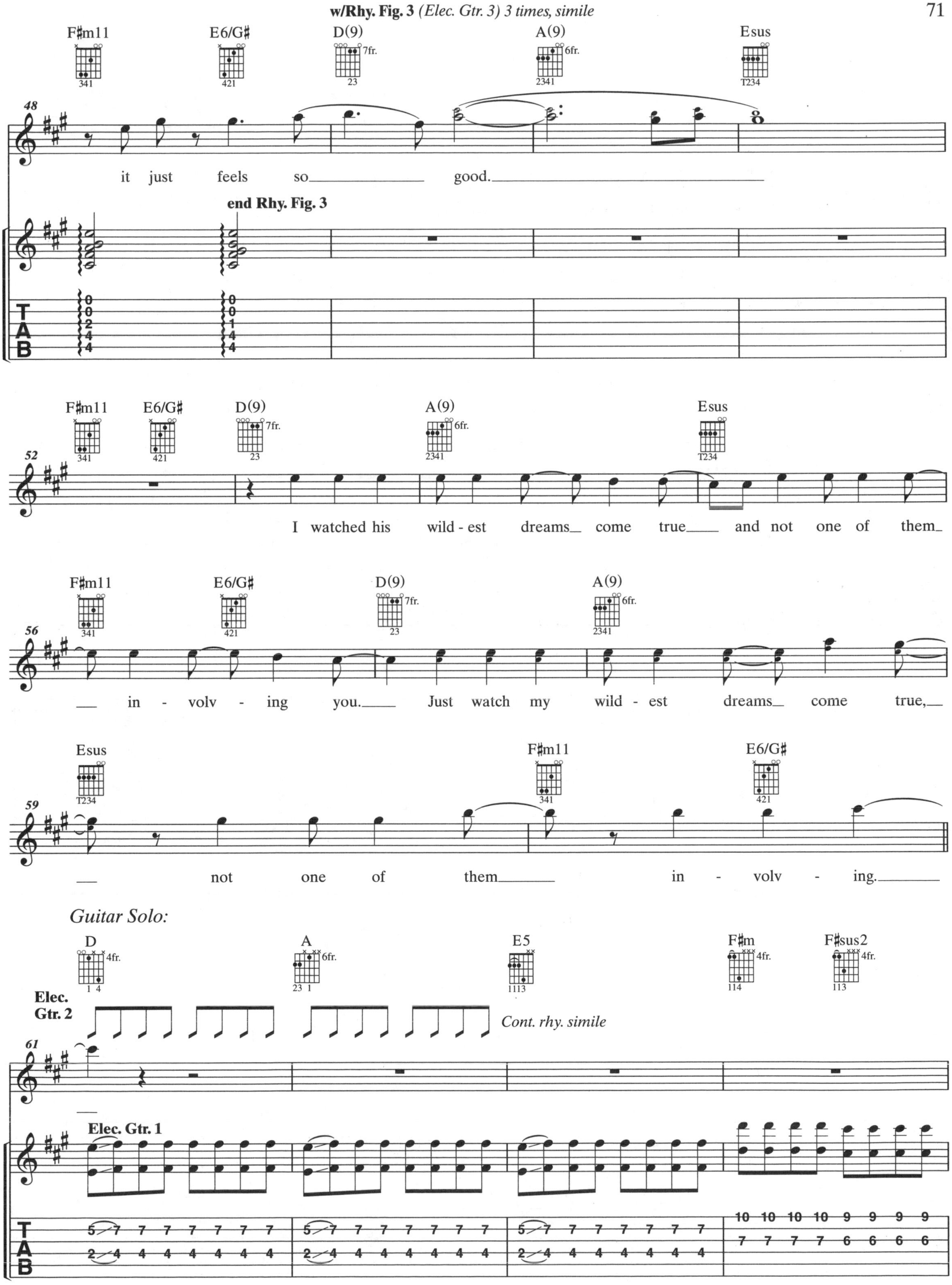
w/Rhy. Fig. 3 (Elec. Gtr. 3) 3 times, simile
F♯m11
E6/G♯
D(9)
A(9)
Esus
it just feels so good.
end Rhy. Fig. 3
I watched his wild - est dreams come true and not one of them
in - volv - ing you. Just watch my wild - est dreams come true,
not one of them in - volv - ing.
Guitar Solo:
D
A
E5
F♯m
F♯sus2
Elec. Gtr. 2
Cont. rhy. simile
Elec. Gtr. 1

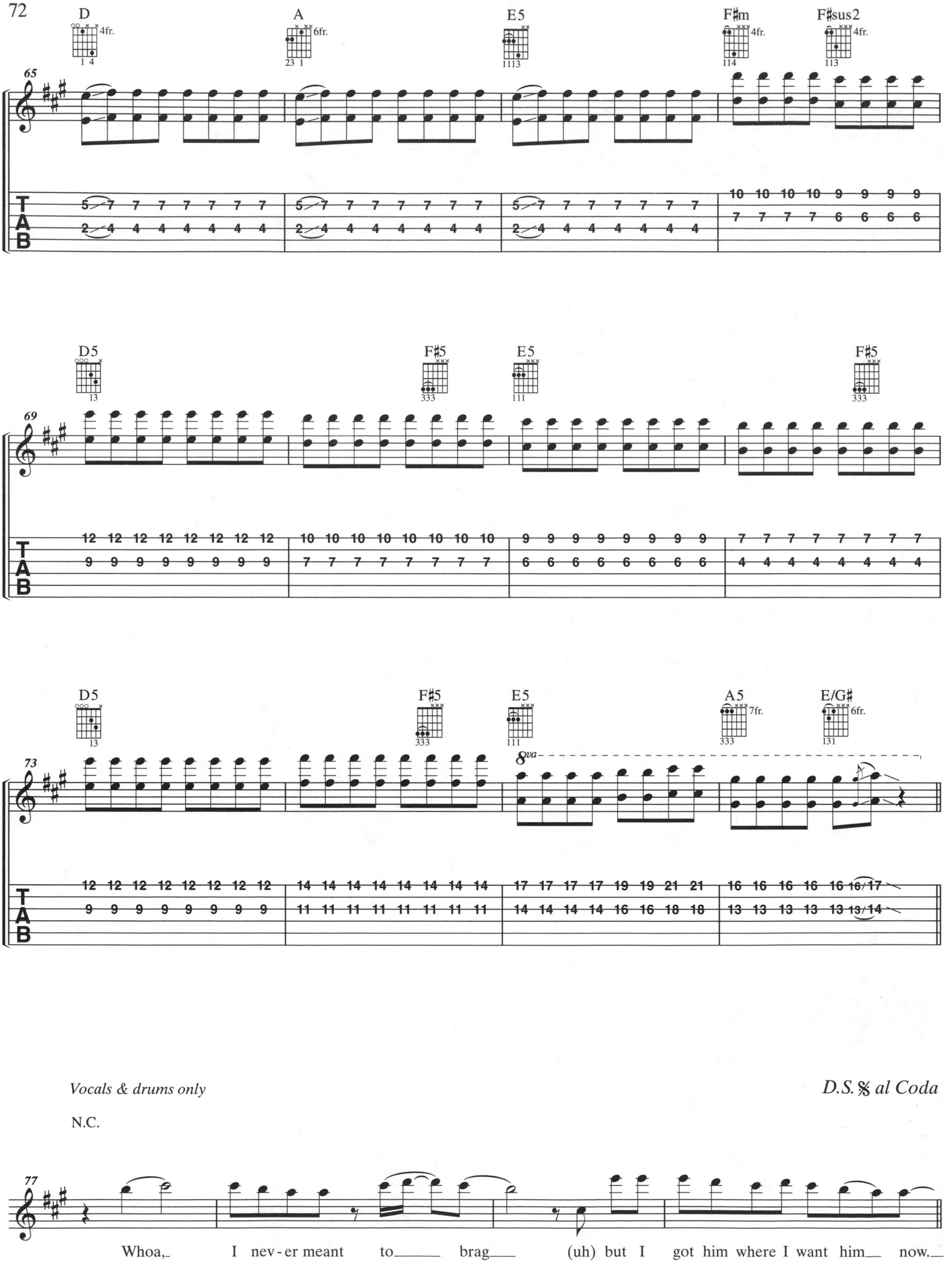
D
A
E5
F♯m
F♯sus2
D5
F♯5
E5
F♯5
D5
F♯5
E5
A5
E/G♯
8va
Vocals & drums only
N.C.
D.S. 𝄋 al Coda
Whoa, I nev-er meant to brag (uh) but I got him where I want him now.

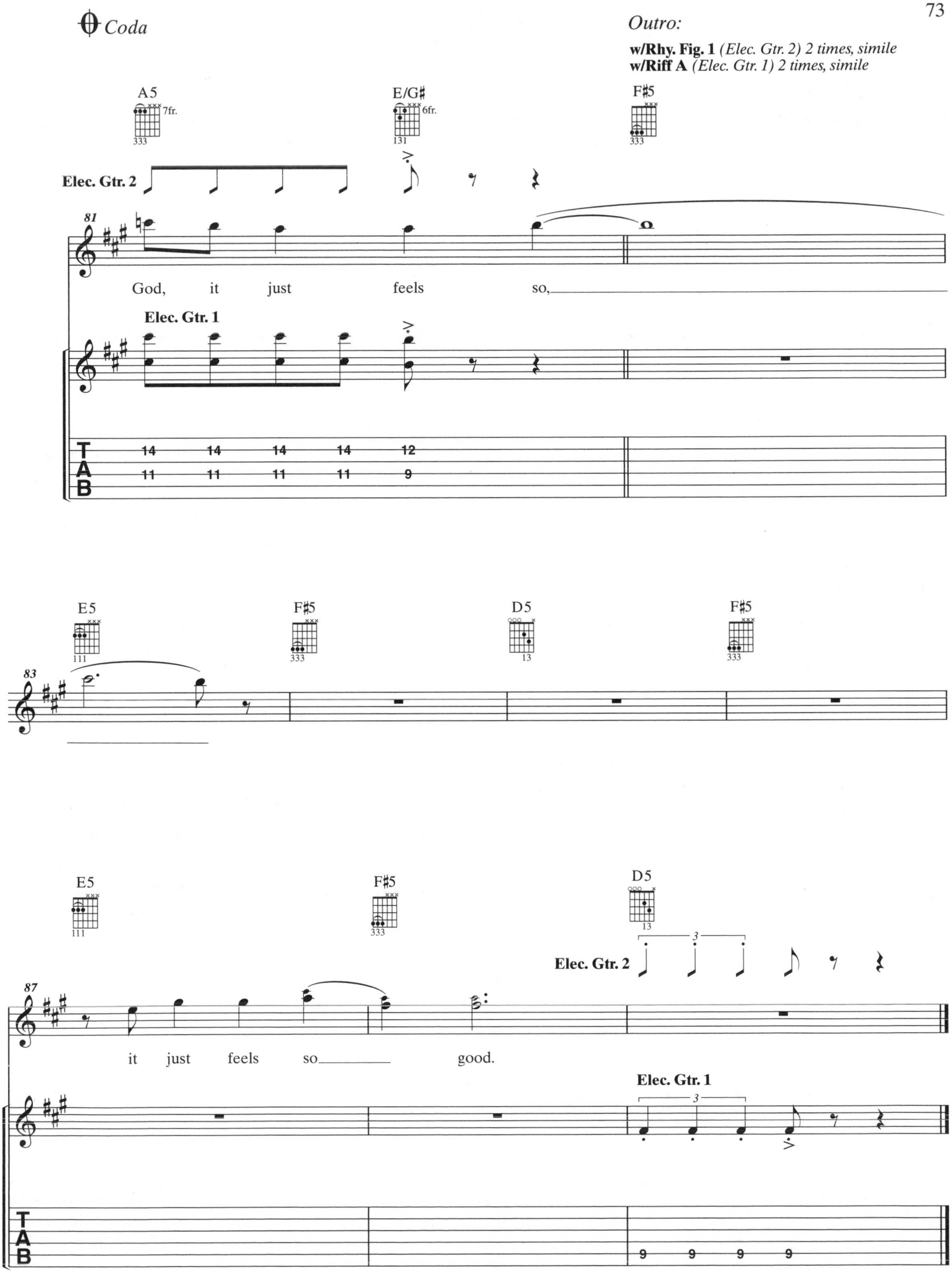
Coda
Outro:
w/Rhy. Fig. 1 (Elec. Gtr. 2) 2 times, simile
w/Riff A (Elec. Gtr. 1) 2 times, simile
A5
7fr.
E/G♯
6fr.
F♯5
Elec. Gtr. 2
God, it just feels so,
Elec. Gtr. 1
E5
F♯5
D5
F♯5
E5
F♯5
D5
Elec. Gtr. 2
it just feels so good.
Elec. Gtr. 1

THAT'S WHAT YOU GET

*All Gtrs. in Drop D tuning, down 1/2 step:
⑥ = D♭ ③ = G♭
⑤ = A♭ ② = B♭
④ = D♭ ① = E♭

Words and Music by
HAYLEY WILLIAMS, JOSH FARRO
and TAYLOR YORK

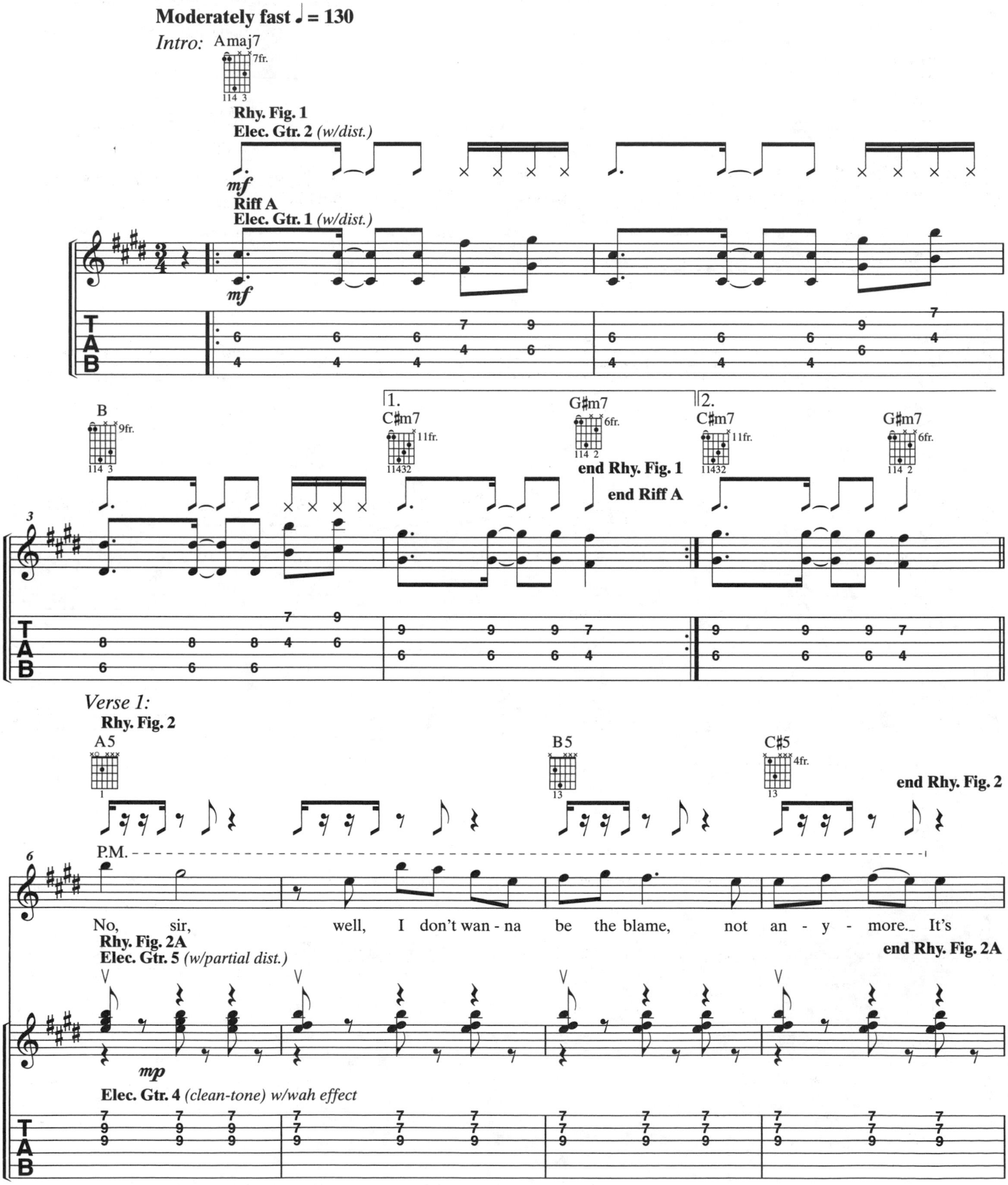

*Recording sounds a half step lower than written.

w/Rhy. Figs. 2 & 2A (Elec. Gtr. 2 & Elec. Gtrs. 3 & 4) simile
A5
B5
C♯5
4fr.
your turn to take a seat, we're set - tl - ing the fi - nal score. And
w/Riff A (Elec. Gtr. 1) simile
w/Rhy. Fig. 1 (Elec. Gtr. 2) simile
Amaj7
7fr.
B
9fr.
C♯m7
11fr.
G♯m7
6fr.
why do we like to hurt so much? I can't
w/Rhy. Figs. 2 & 2A (Elec. Gtr. 2 & Elec. Gtrs. 3 & 4) 2 times, simile
A5
B5
C♯5
4fr.
de - cide. You have made it hard - er just to go on. And
A5
B5
why? All the pos - si - bil - i - ties, well,
C♯5
4fr.
E
Elec. Gtr. 2 dbld.
I was wrong.
Chorus:
A5
7fr.
E5
C♯m
11fr.
B5
9fr.
Elec. Gtr. 2
That's what you get when you've let your heart win. Whoa!
Elec. Gtr. 5 (w/partial dist.)
8va
mf
hold throughout
T
A
B

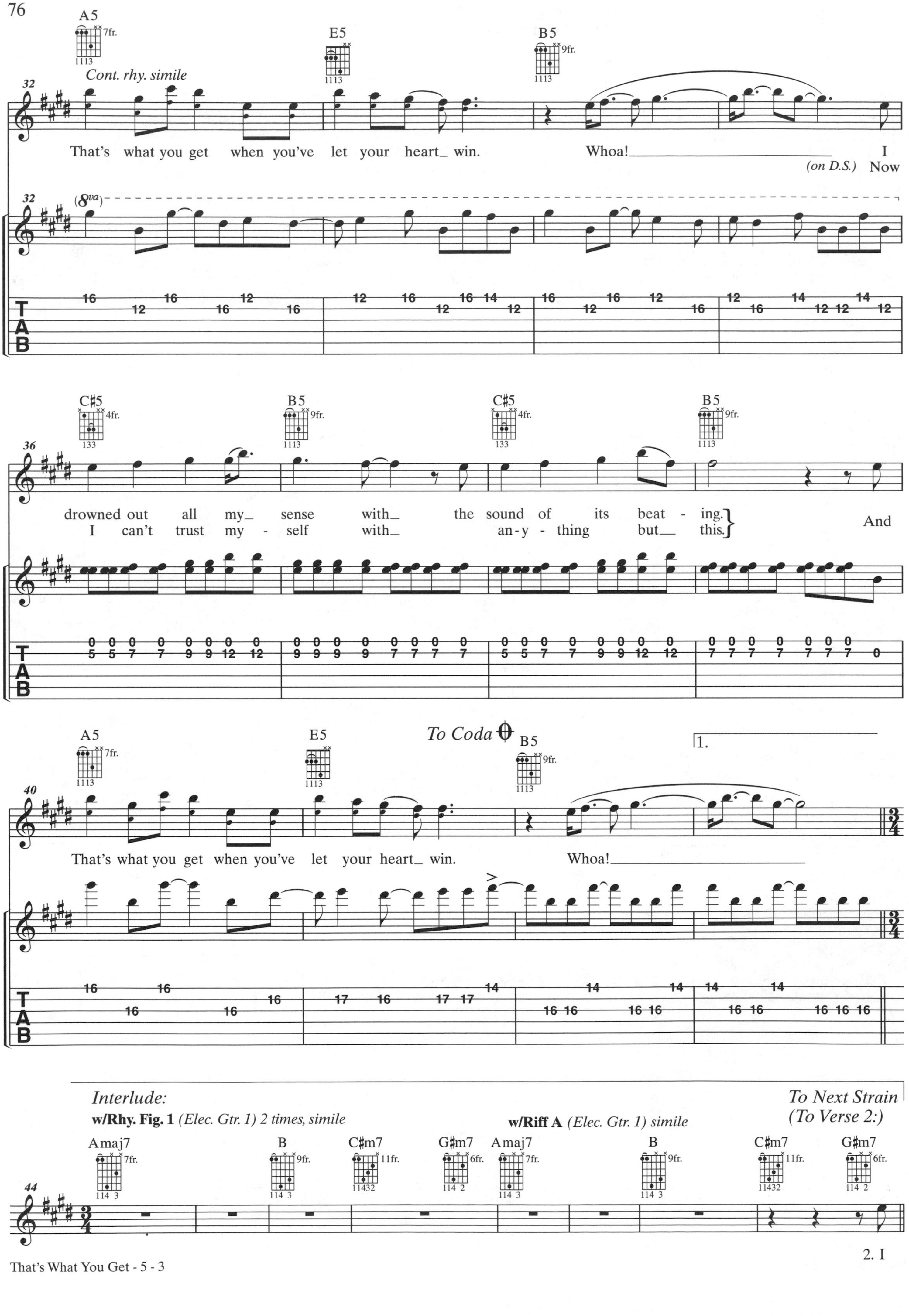
A5
E5
B5
Cont. rhy. simile
That's what you get when you've let your heart_ win. Whoa!_ I
(on D.S.) Now
(8va)
C♯5
B5
drowned out all my_ sense with_ the sound of its beat - ing.
I can't trust my - self with_ an-y - thing but_ this.
And
To Coda
1.
That's what you get when you've let your heart_ win. Whoa!_
Interlude:
w/Rhy. Fig. 1 (Elec. Gtr. 1) 2 times, simile
w/Riff A (Elec. Gtr. 1) simile
To Next Strain (To Verse 2:)
Amaj7
B
C♯m7
G♯m7
2. I

2.3.
Verses 2 & 3:
w/Rhy. Figs. 2 & 2A (Elec. Gtr. 2 & Elec. Gtrs. 3 & 4) 4 times, simile
A5 B5 C♯5 E
Amaj7 B C♯m7 G♯m7
wonder how am I supposed to feel when you're not here. 'Cause I burned ev'ry bridge I ever built when you were here. I still try holding on to silly things. I never learn. Oh, why? All the possibilities, I'm sure you've heard.
3. Pain, make your way to me, to me. And I'll always be just so inviting. If I ever start to think straight, this heart will start a riot in me. Let's start, start. Hey!
Elec. Gtr. 2 dbld.
D.S. 𝄋
w/Riff A (Elec. Gtr. 1) 2 times, simile
w/Rhy. Fig. 1 (Elec. Gtr. 2) 2 times, simile
Why do we like to hurt so much? Oh, why do we like to hurt so much?

B5
D.S. 𝄋 al Coda
A capella
Elec. Gtr. 2
P.M.
80
That's what you get when you've let your heart_ win. Whoa!
𝄌 Coda
B5
9fr.
Amaj7
7fr.
Elec. Gtr. 2
84
Whoa!
Elec. Gtr. 1
hold
E
87
harm.

SO HAPPY

Lyrics by TYLER CONNOLLY
Music by TYLER CONNOLLY,
DAVID BRENNER and DEAN BACK

*All Gtrs. in Drop D tuning, down 1/2 step:

⑥ = D♭ ③ = G♭
⑤ = A♭ ② = B♭
④ = D♭ ① = E♭

Moderate rock ♩ = 133
Intro:

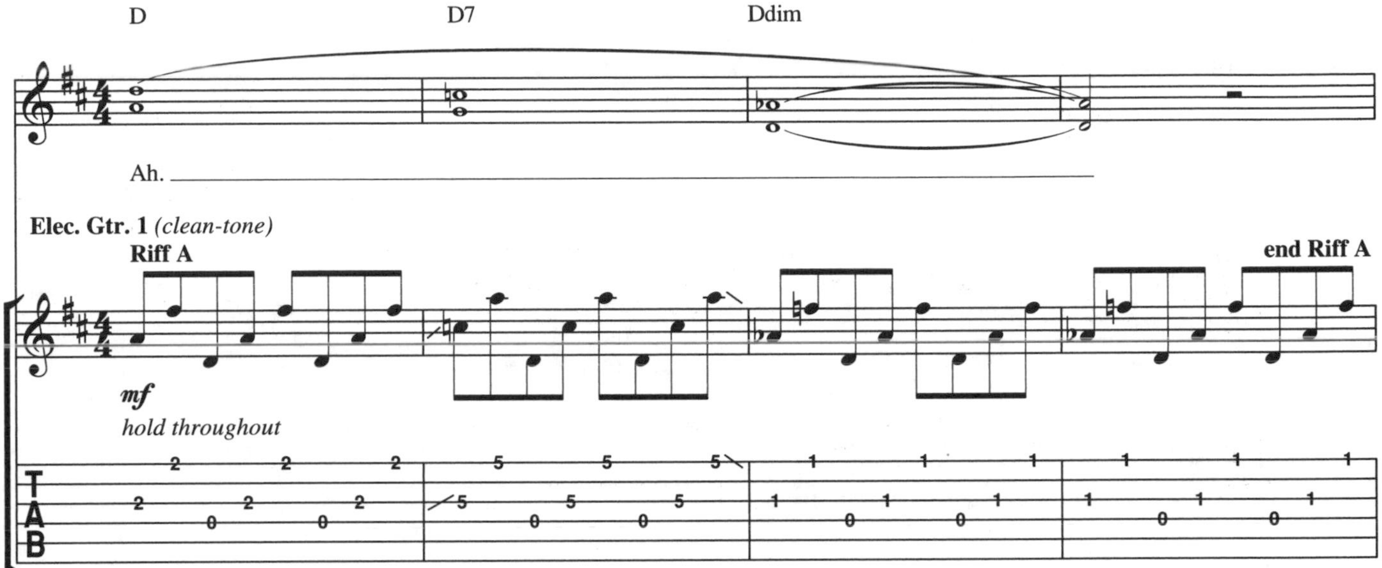

*Recording sounds a half step lower than written.

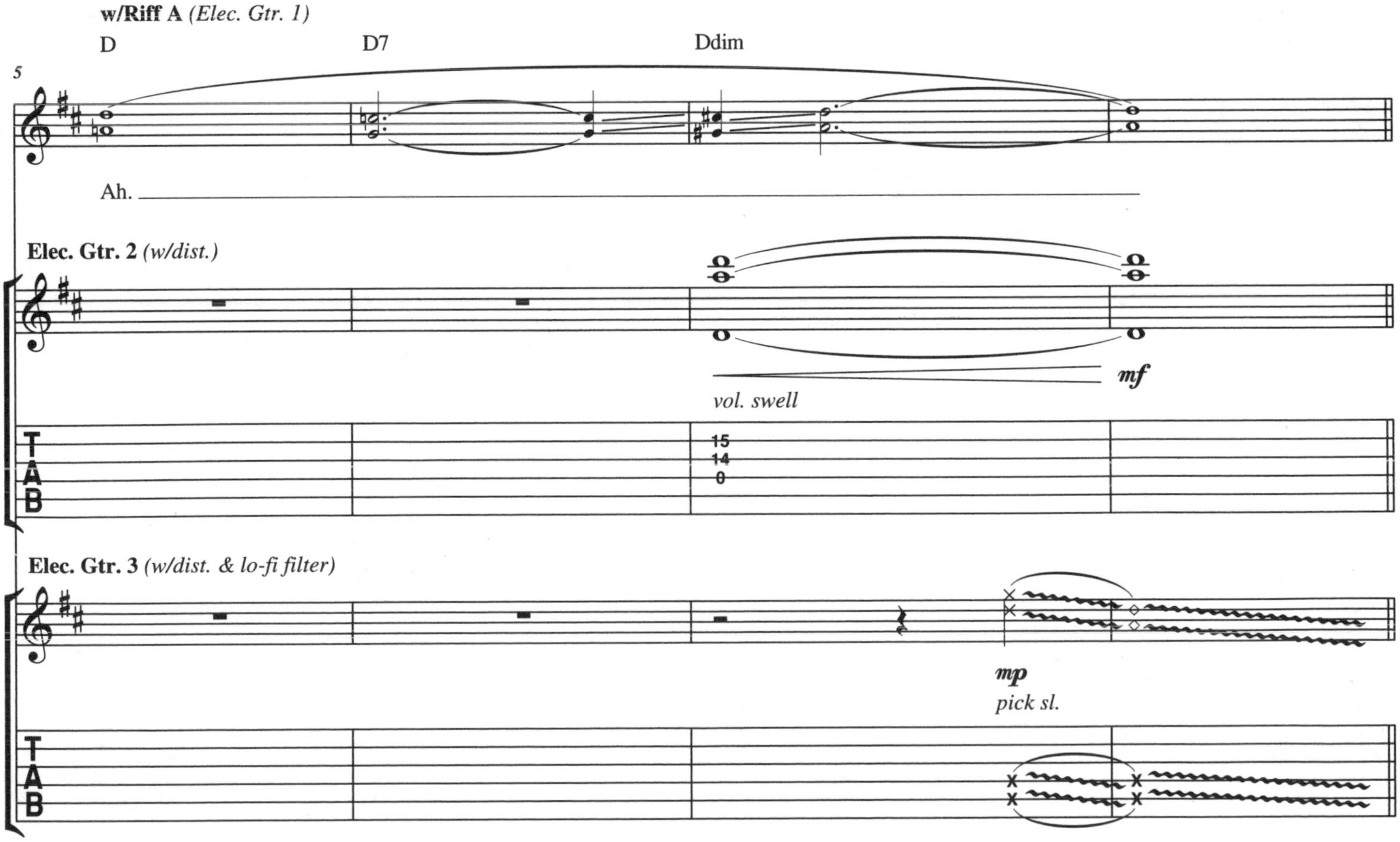

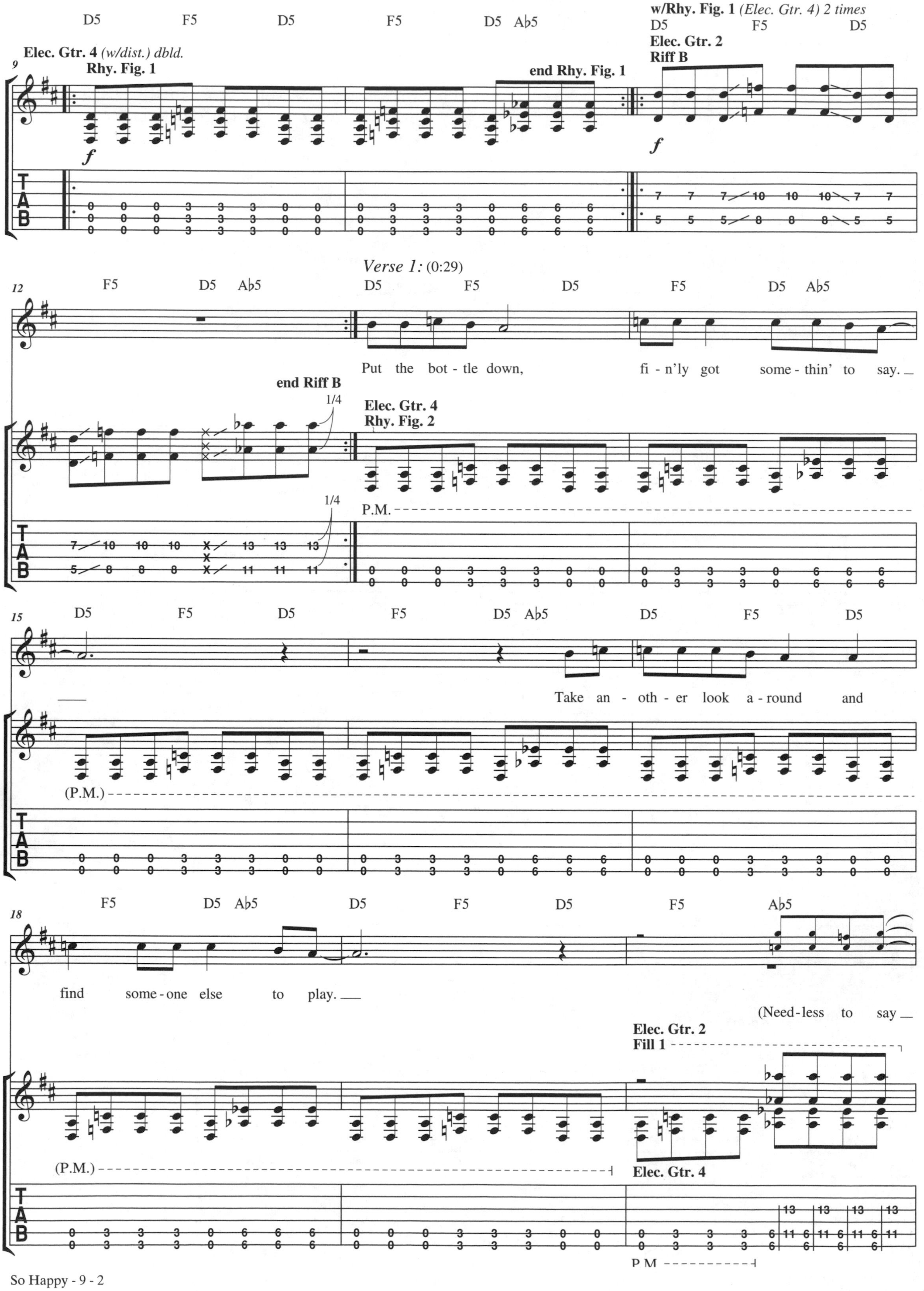
w/Rhy. Fig. 1 (Elec. Gtr. 4) 2 times
Elec. Gtr. 4 (w/dist.) dbld.
Rhy. Fig. 1
end Rhy. Fig. 1
Elec. Gtr. 2
Riff B
D5 F5 D5 F5 D5 Ab5
Verse 1: (0:29)
Put the bot - tle down, fi - n'ly got some - thin' to say.
end Riff B
Elec. Gtr. 4
Rhy. Fig. 2
P.M.
Take an - oth - er look a - round and
(P.M.)
find some - one else to play.
(Need - less to say
Elec. Gtr. 2
Fill 1
Elec. Gtr. 4

w/Fill 1 (Elec. Gtr. 2)
D5 F5 D5 F5 A♭5 D5 F5 D5
that you've got prob - lems. that I'm gon - na solve
)
(There's no f*** - in' way.)
Elec. Gtr. 4
P.M.
P.M.
w/Fill 1 (Elec. Gtr. 2)
F5 A♭5 D5 F5 D5 F5 D5 A♭5
'em. Ev - 'ry time you slip, then you fall
(It's nev - er the same.)
(P.M.)
P.M.
D5 F5 D5 F5 D5 A♭5 G5 A♭5
down, down, down. Ev - er won - der what I've
T
A
B

30
G5
F5
been think - in' a - bout?
I've been think - in' 'bout throw - in' you out.
end Rhy. Fig. 2
T
A
B
𝄋 Chorus: (1:05), (2:13)
D5
F5
C5
33
I'm so hap - py, how 'bout you?
Voc. Fig. 1
I'm fed up,
Rhy. Fig. 3
36
F5
D5
F5
C5
I'm so hap - py now we're through.
so get up and get out.
end Voc. Fig. 1

w/Voc. Fig. 1
F5
D5
C5
I was so a - fraid, now you're
Voc. Fig. 2
Ah.
Gadd4/B
B♭5
F5
D5
gone a - way. Sent you pack - in', look who's laugh - in' now.
end Voc. Fig. 2
F5
C5
I'm so hap - py that I feel this way. I'm so

w/Rhy. Fig. 1 (Elec. Gtr. 4)
w/Riff B (Elec. Gtr. 2)
To Coda
D5 F5 D5 F5 D5 A♭5
48
hap - py that I threw you a - way.
end Rhy. Fig. 3
T
A
B
5 5 3 5 5 3 5 5 3 5 5 3 5 5 3 5 5 3 5 5 3 5 5 3
Verse 2: (1:37)
w/Rhy. Fig. 2 (Elec. Gtr. 4)
w/Riff B (*Elec. Gtr. 3) 8 times
51
D5 F5 D5 F5 D5 A♭5 D5 F5 D5 F5 D5 A♭5
Put your prob - lems down and pick up what's left of the pain, and take a
*w/delay & reverb
w/Fill 1 (Elec. Gtr. 2)
55
D5 F5 D5 F5 D5 A♭5 D5 F5 D5 F5 A♭5
good look at your - self and see who's real - ly to blame.
(Need - less to say,
w/Fill 1 (Elec. Gtr. 2)
59
D5 F5 D5 F5 A♭5 D5 F5 D5
you've got is - sues. that I'm gon - na fix
) (There's no f*** - in' way.)
w/Fill 1 (Elec. Gtr. 2)
62
F5 A♭5 D5 F5 D5 F5 D5 A♭5
you. ev - er since you had fall - en
(It's nev - er the same.)
65
D5 F5 D5 F5 D5 A♭5 G5 A♭5
down, down, down. Ev - er won - der what I've

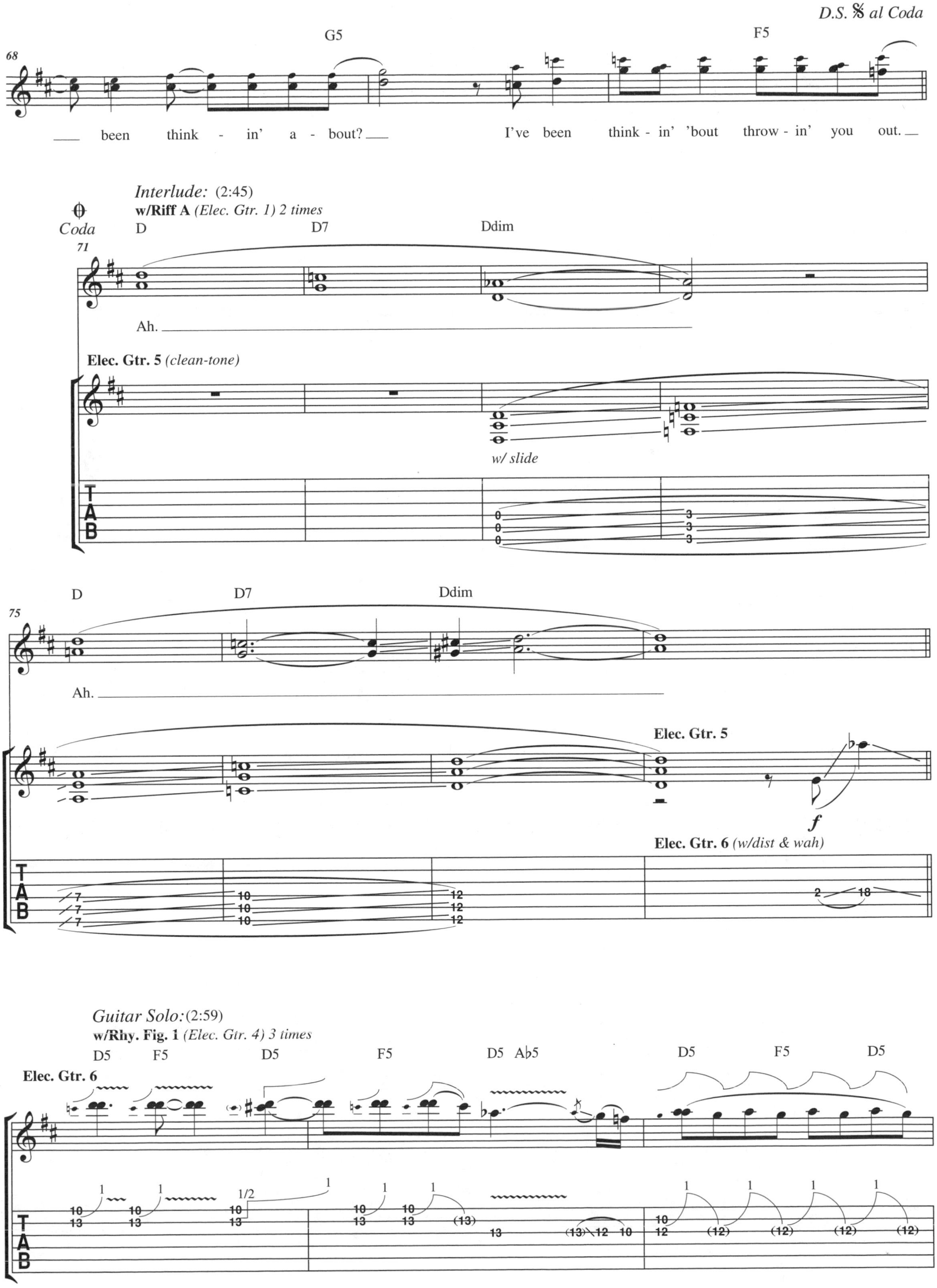
D.S. 𝄋 al Coda
G5
F5
68
been think - in' a - bout?
I've been think - in' 'bout throw - in' you out.
Interlude: (2:45)
w/Riff A (Elec. Gtr. 1) 2 times
Coda
D
D7
Ddim
71
Ah.
Elec. Gtr. 5 (clean-tone)
w/ slide
75
Elec. Gtr. 5
f
Elec. Gtr. 6 (w/dist & wah)
Guitar Solo: (2:59)
w/Rhy. Fig. 1 (Elec. Gtr. 4) 3 times
D5
F5
D5
F5
D5 A♭5
Elec. Gtr. 6

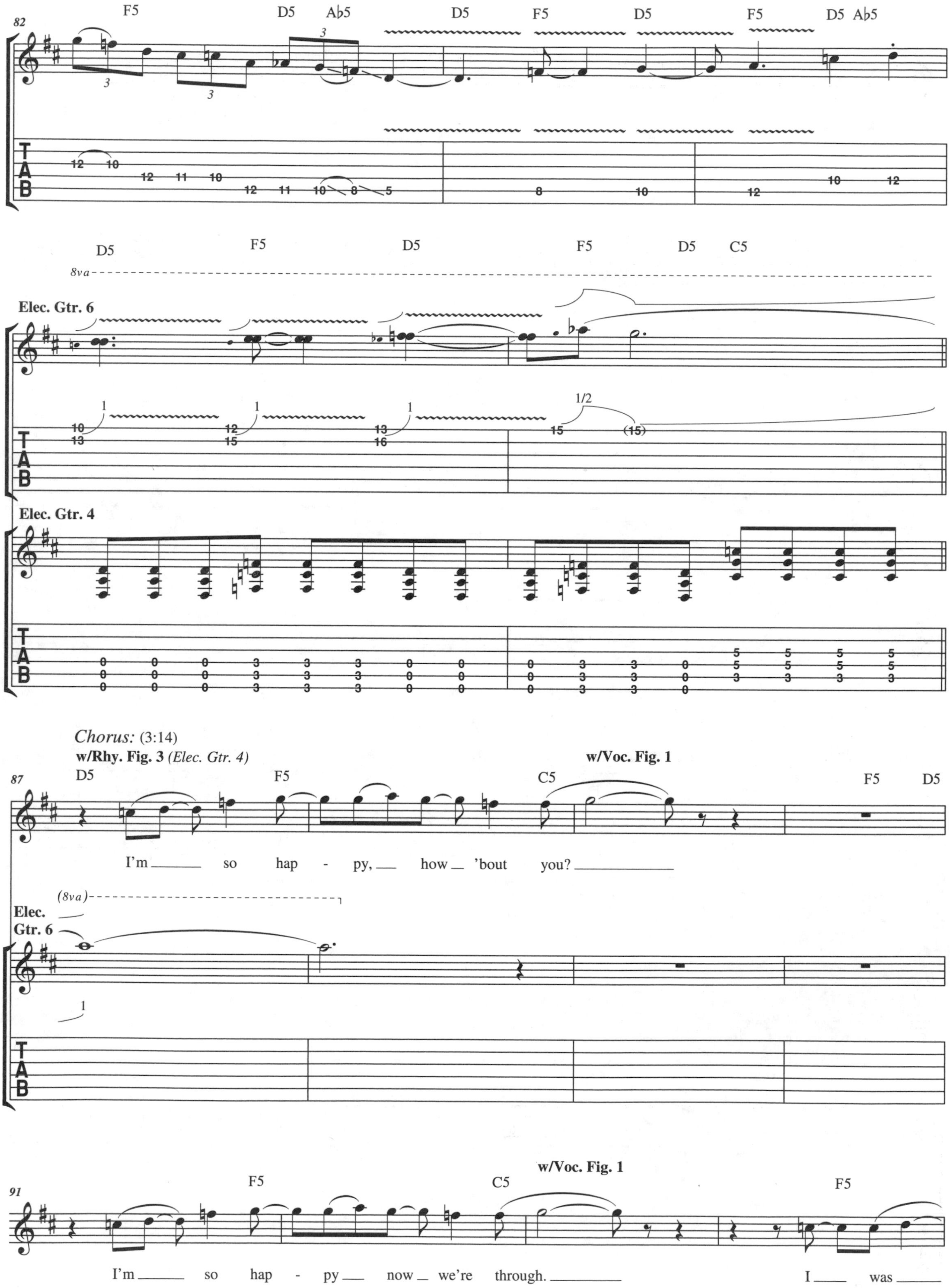
F5 D5 A♭5 D5 F5 D5 F5 D5 A♭5
D5 F5 D5 F5 D5 C5
8va
Elec. Gtr. 6
1/2
Elec. Gtr. 4
Chorus: (3:14)
w/Rhy. Fig. 3 (Elec. Gtr. 4)
w/Voc. Fig. 1
D5 F5 C5 F5 D5
I'm so hap - py, how 'bout you?
(8va)
Elec. Gtr. 6
w/Voc. Fig. 1
F5 C5 F5
I'm so hap - py now we're through. I was

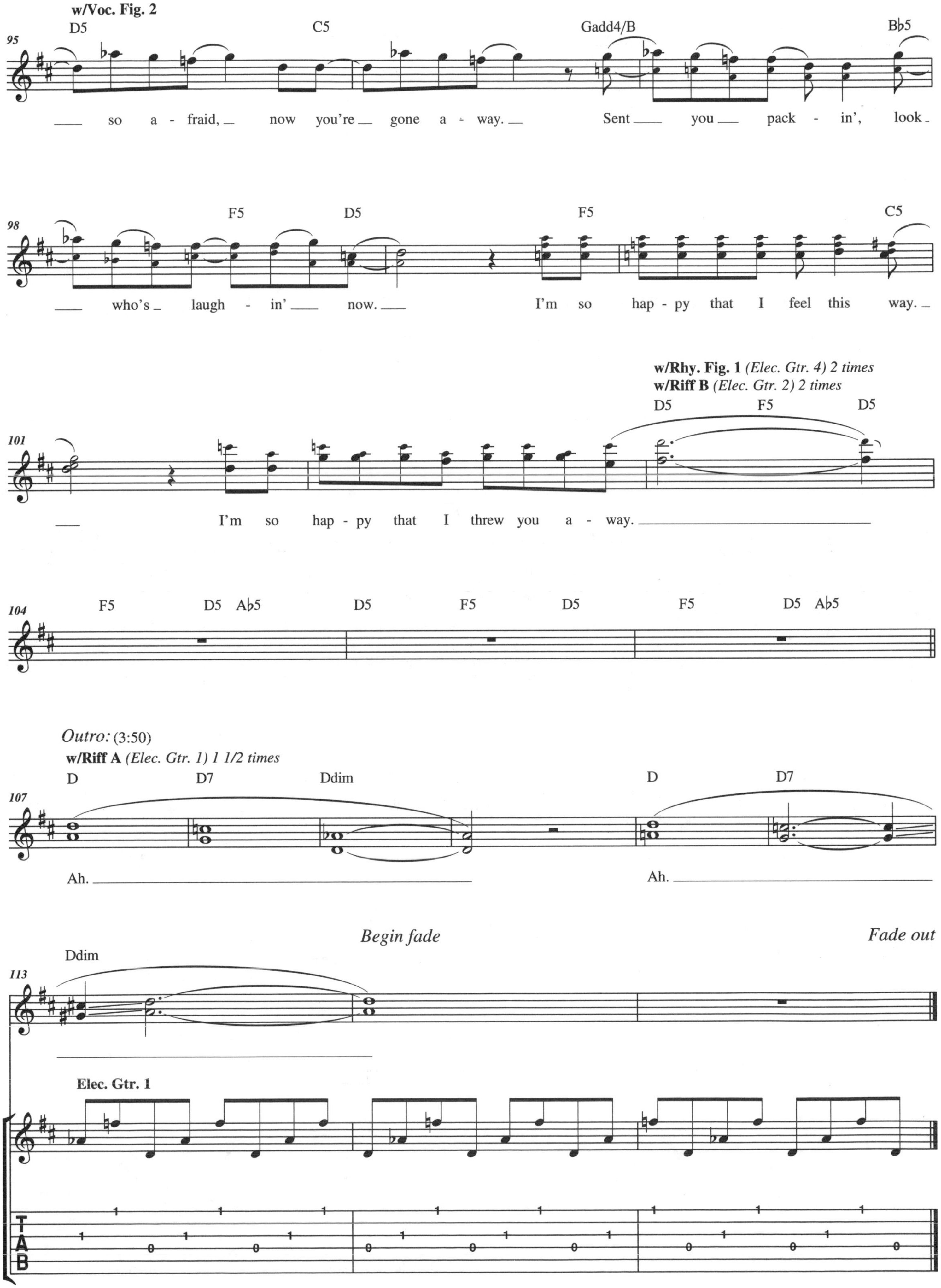
w/Voc. Fig. 2
D5 C5 Gadd4/B B♭5
so a - fraid, now you're gone a - way. Sent you pack - in', look
F5 D5 F5 C5
who's laugh - in' now. I'm so hap - py that I feel this way.
w/Rhy. Fig. 1 (Elec. Gtr. 4) 2 times
w/Riff B (Elec. Gtr. 2) 2 times
D5 F5 D5
I'm so hap - py that I threw you a - way.
F5 D5 A♭5 D5 F5 D5 F5 D5 A♭5
Outro: (3:50)
w/Riff A (Elec. Gtr. 1) 1 1/2 times
D D7 Ddim D D7
Ah. Ah.
Begin fade
Fade out
Ddim
Elec. Gtr. 1
T
A
B

ALL OR NOTHING

Lyrics by TYLER CONNOLLY
Music by TYLER CONNOLLY,
DAVID BRENNER and DEAN BACK

*All Gtrs. tune down 1/2 step:

⑥ = E♭ ③ = G♭
⑤ = A♭ ② = B♭
④ = D♭ ① = E♭

Moderately ♩ = 78

Intro:

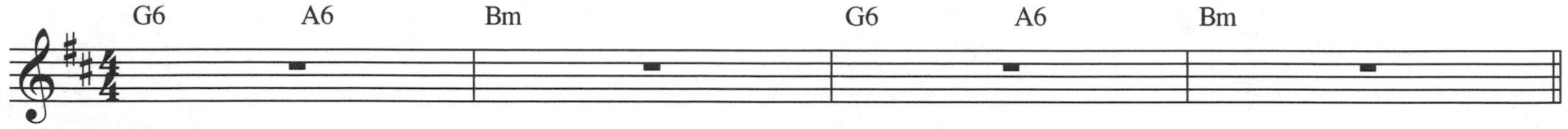
G6
A6
Bm
G6
A6
Bm

*Recording sounds a half step lower than written.

Verse 1: (0:13)

Bm(11)
1342
D
132
A
111
Elec. Gtr. 1 (w/light dist.)
Rhy. Fig. 1
end Rhy. Fig. 1
mf
5
When I first saw you stand - in' there, you know, was a lit - tle hard not to stare.

Bm(11)
1342
D
132
A
111
7
So ner - vous when I drove you home, I know being a - part's a lit - tle hard to bear.

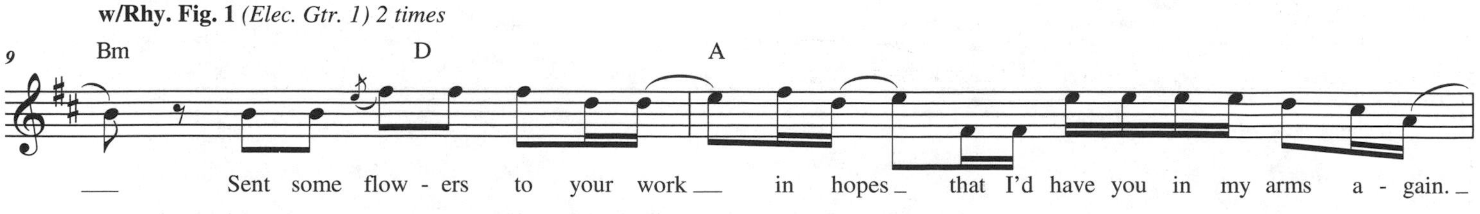
w/Rhy. Fig. 1 (Elec. Gtr. 1) 2 times
9
Bm
D
A
Sent some flow - ers to your work in hopes that I'd have you in my arms a - gain.

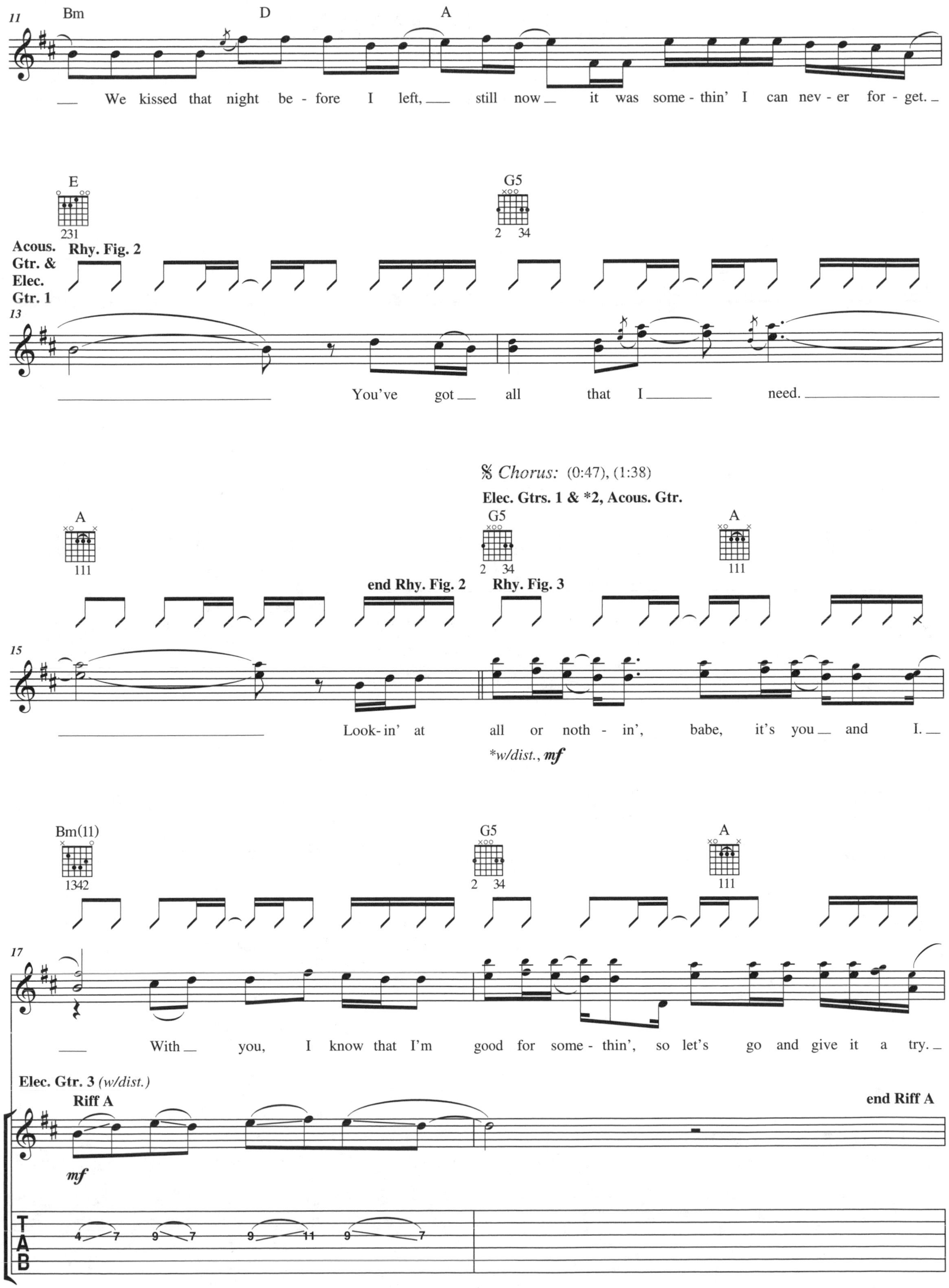
11
Bm D A
We kissed that night be - fore I left, still now it was some - thin' I can nev - er for - get.
E
231
G5
2 34
Acous. Gtr. & Elec. Gtr. 1
Rhy. Fig. 2
13
You've got all that I need.
𝄋 Chorus: (0:47), (1:38)
Elec. Gtrs. 1 & *2, Acous. Gtr.
A
111
G5
2 34
A
111
end Rhy. Fig. 2
Rhy. Fig. 3
15
Look- in' at all or noth - in', babe, it's you and I.
*w/dist., mf
Bm(11)
1342
G5
2 34
A
111
17
With you, I know that I'm good for some - thin', so let's go and give it a try.
Elec. Gtr. 3 (w/dist.)
Riff A
end Riff A
mf
T A B
4 7 9 7 9 11 9 7

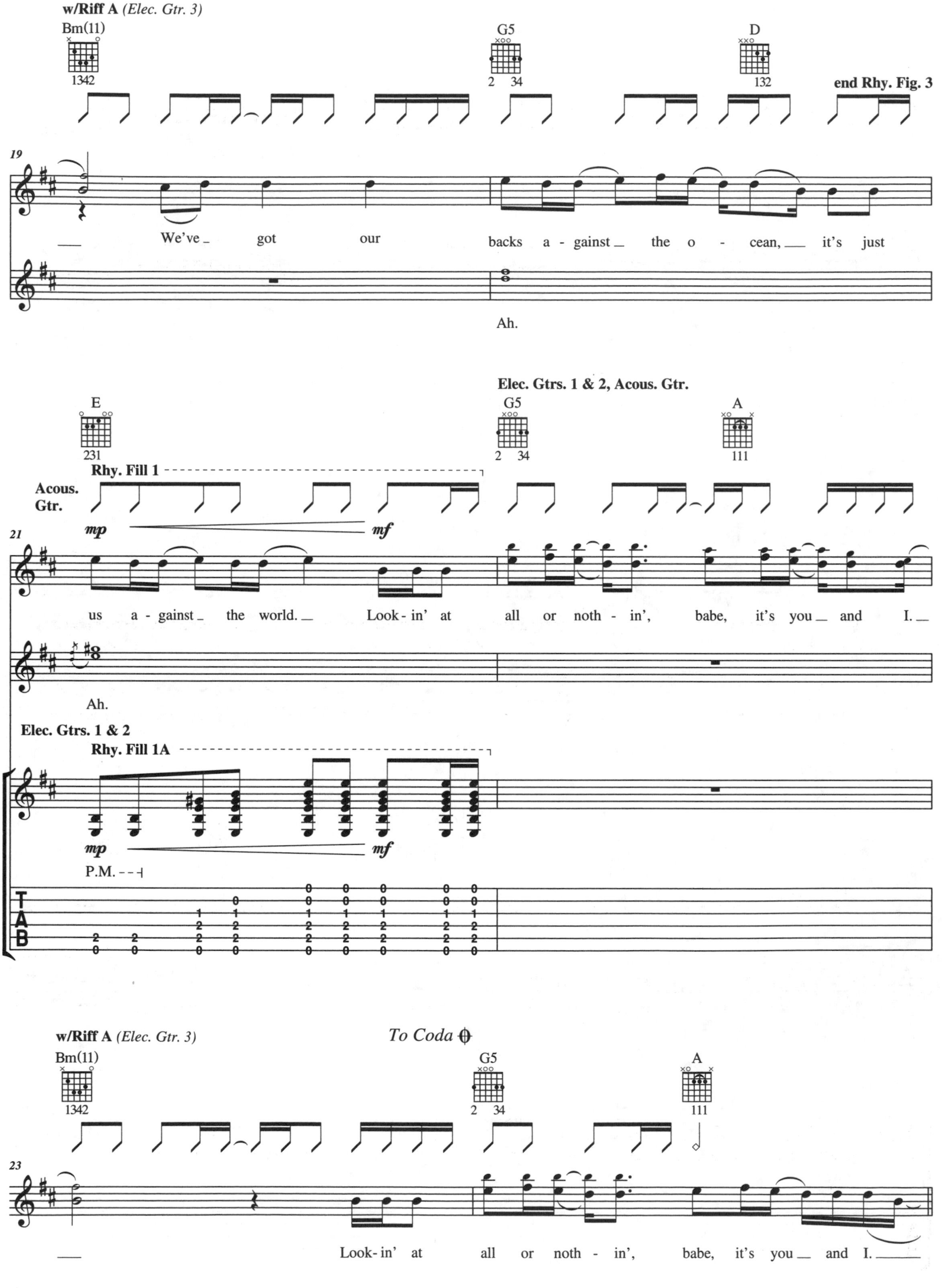
w/Riff A (Elec. Gtr. 3)
Bm(11)
1342
G5
2 34
D
132
end Rhy. Fig. 3
19
We've _ got our backs a - gainst _ the o - cean, ___ it's just
Ah.
Elec. Gtrs. 1 & 2, Acous. Gtr.
E
231
G5
2 34
A
111
Rhy. Fill 1
Acous. Gtr.
21
mp
mf
us a - gainst _ the world. _ Look - in' at all or noth - in', babe, it's you _ and I. _
Ah.
Elec. Gtrs. 1 & 2
Rhy. Fill 1A
mp
mf
P.M.
T
A
B
w/Riff A (Elec. Gtr. 3)
To Coda
Bm(11)
1342
G5
2 34
A
111
23
Look - in' at all or noth - in', babe, it's you _ and I. ___

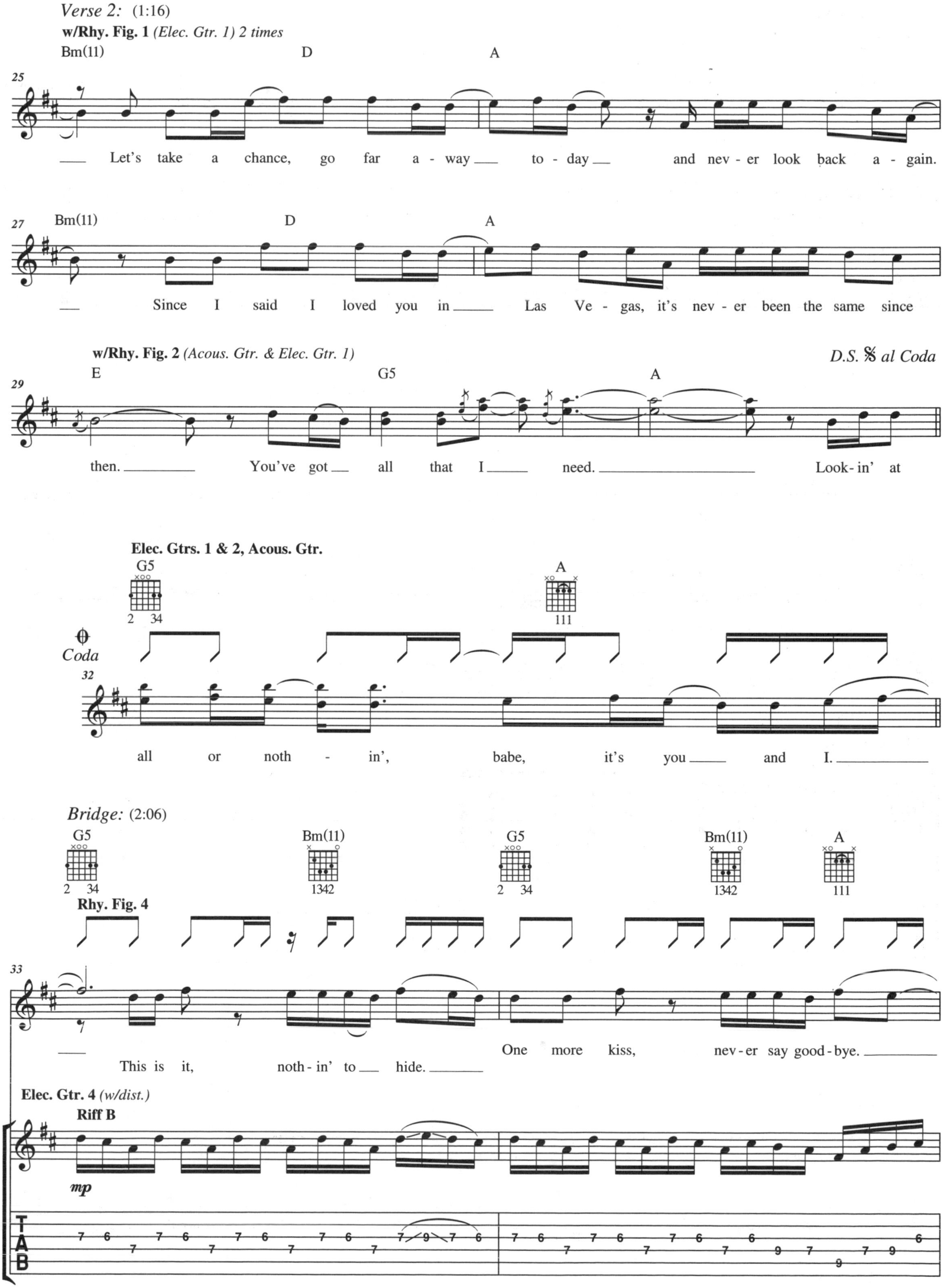
Verse 2: (1:16)
w/Rhy. Fig. 1 (Elec. Gtr. 1) 2 times
Bm(11) D A
25
Let's take a chance, go far a - way to - day and nev - er look back a - gain.
27
Bm(11) D A
Since I said I loved you in Las Ve - gas, it's nev - er been the same since
w/Rhy. Fig. 2 (Acous. Gtr. & Elec. Gtr. 1)
D.S. 𝄋 al Coda
29
E G5 A
then. You've got all that I need. Look- in' at
Elec. Gtrs. 1 & 2, Acous. Gtr.
G5
2 34
A
111
Coda
32
all or noth - in', babe, it's you and I.
Bridge: (2:06)
G5 Bm(11) G5 Bm(11) A
2 34 1342 2 34 1342 111
Rhy. Fig. 4
33
This is it, noth - in' to hide.
One more kiss, nev - er say good - bye.
Elec. Gtr. 4 (w/dist.)
Riff B
mp
T
A
B
7 6 7 7 6 7 7 6 7 7 6 7 7 9 7 6
7 6 7 7 6 7 7 6 7 6 9 7 9 7 9 6

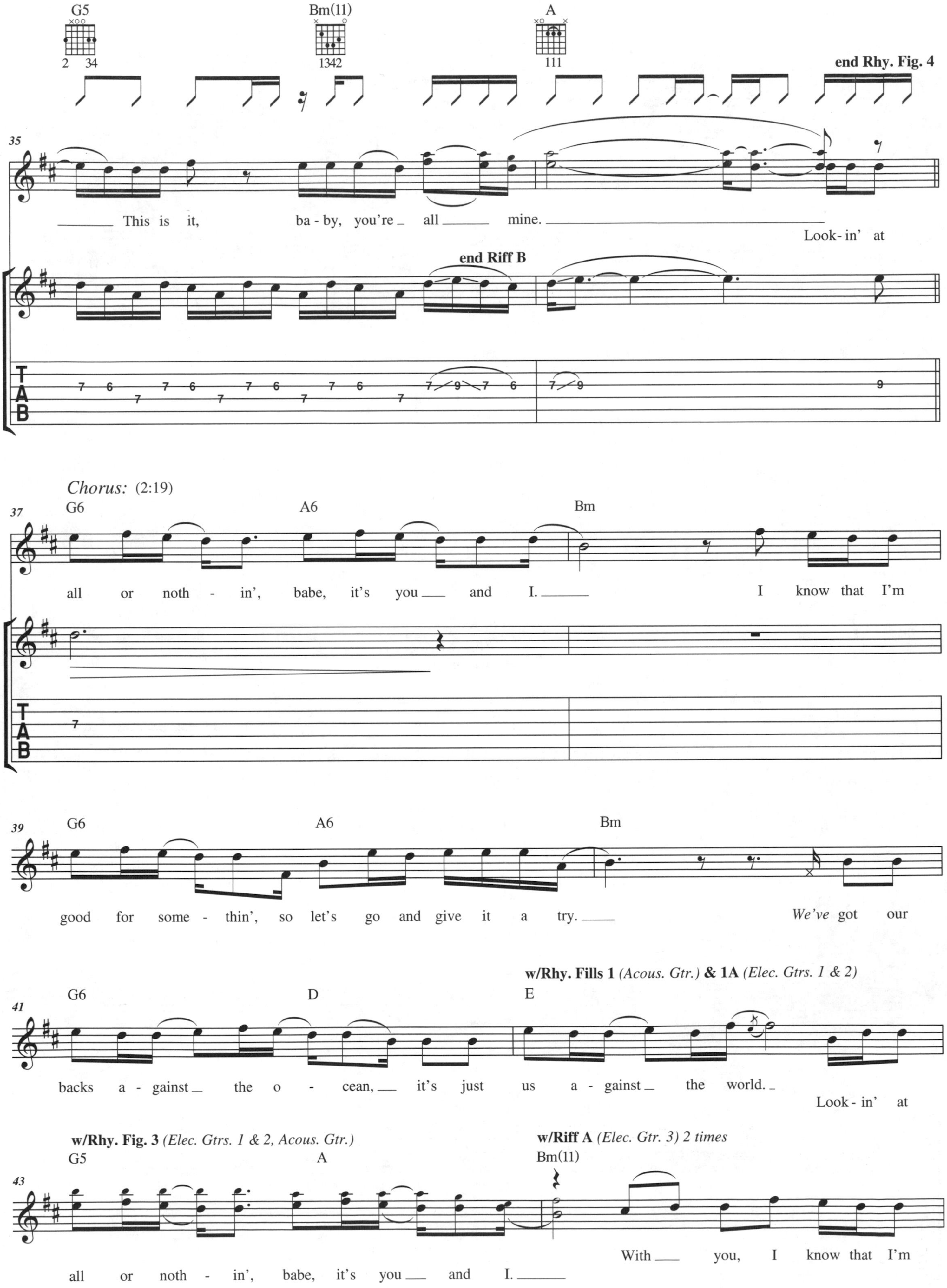
G5 Bm(11) A
end Rhy. Fig. 4
This is it, ba - by, you're all mine. Look - in' at
end Riff B
Chorus: (2:19)
G6 A6 Bm
all or noth - in', babe, it's you and I. I know that I'm
G6 A6 Bm
good for some - thin', so let's go and give it a try. We've got our
w/Rhy. Fills 1 (Acous. Gtr.) & 1A (Elec. Gtrs. 1 & 2)
G6 D E
backs a - gainst the o - cean, it's just us a - gainst the world. Look - in' at
w/Rhy. Fig. 3 (Elec. Gtrs. 1 & 2, Acous. Gtr.)
G5 A
w/Riff A (Elec. Gtr. 3) 2 times
Bm(11)
all or noth - in', babe, it's you and I. With you, I know that I'm

G5
A
Bm(11)
45
good for some - thin', so let's go and give it a try.
We've got our
w/Rhy. Fills 1 (Acous. Gtr.) & 1A (Elec. Gtrs. 1 & 2)
G5
D
E
47
backs a - gainst the o - cean, it's just us a - gainst the world. Look - in' at
Ah.
Ah.
w/Rhy. Fig. 3 (Elec. Gtrs. 1 & 2, Acous. Gtr.) first 3 meas.
w/Riff A (Elec. Gtr. 3)
G5
A
Bm(11)
49
all or noth - in', babe, it's you and I.
Look - in' at
Outro: (3:06)
w/Rhy. Fig. 4 (Elec. Gtrs. 1 & 2, Acous. Gtr.)
w/Riff B (Elec. Gtr. 4)
G5
A
G5
Bm(11)
G5
Bm(11)
A
51
all or noth - in', babe, it's you and I.
Babe, it's you and I,
G5
Bm(11)
A
Bm(11)
1342
Elec. Gtrs. 1 & 2, Acous. Gtr.
54
I.
Elec. Gtr. 5 (w/dist.)
mp
Elec. Gtr. 5
Elec. Gtr. 4

BAD GIRLFRIEND

Lyrics by TYLER CONNOLLY and CHRISTINE CONNOLLY
Music by TYLER CONNOLLY, DAVID BRENNER
and DEAN BACK

*All Gtrs. tune down 1 whole step:

⑥ = D ③ = F
⑤ = G ② = A
④ = C ① = D

Moderately ♩ = 135
Intro:

D5

*Recording sounds a whole step lower than written.

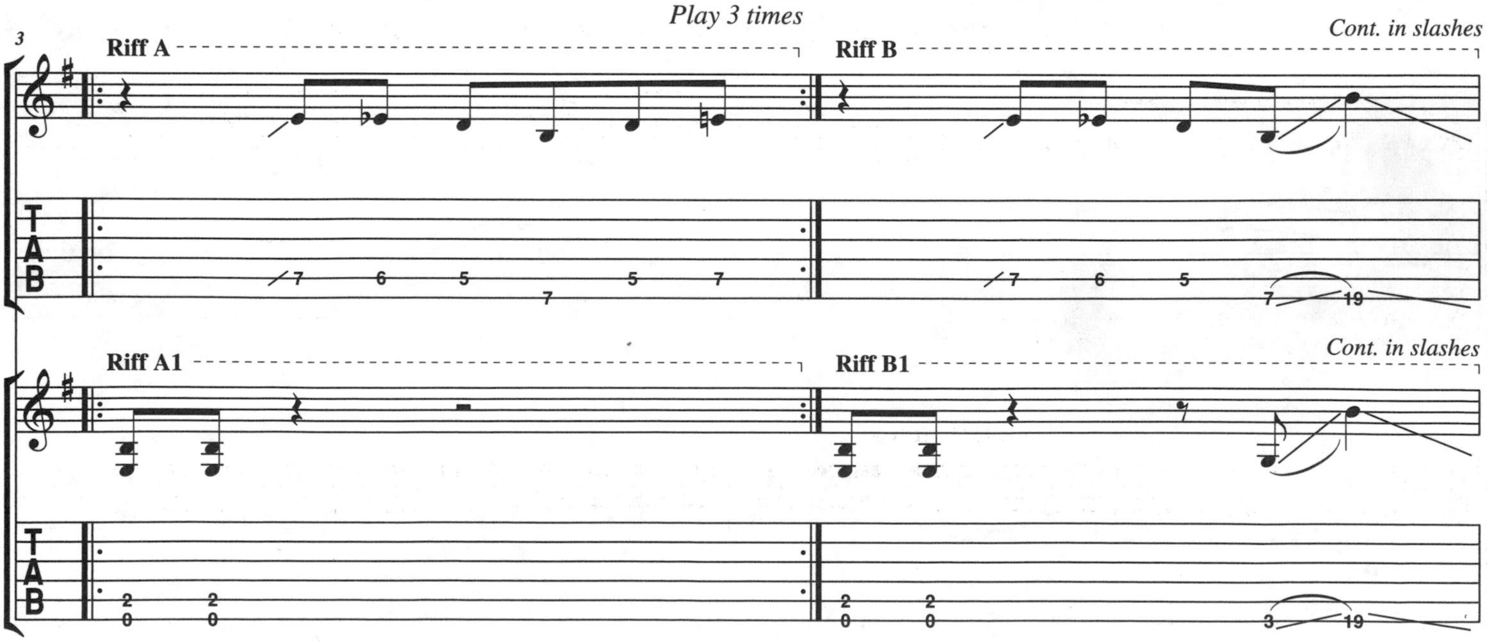

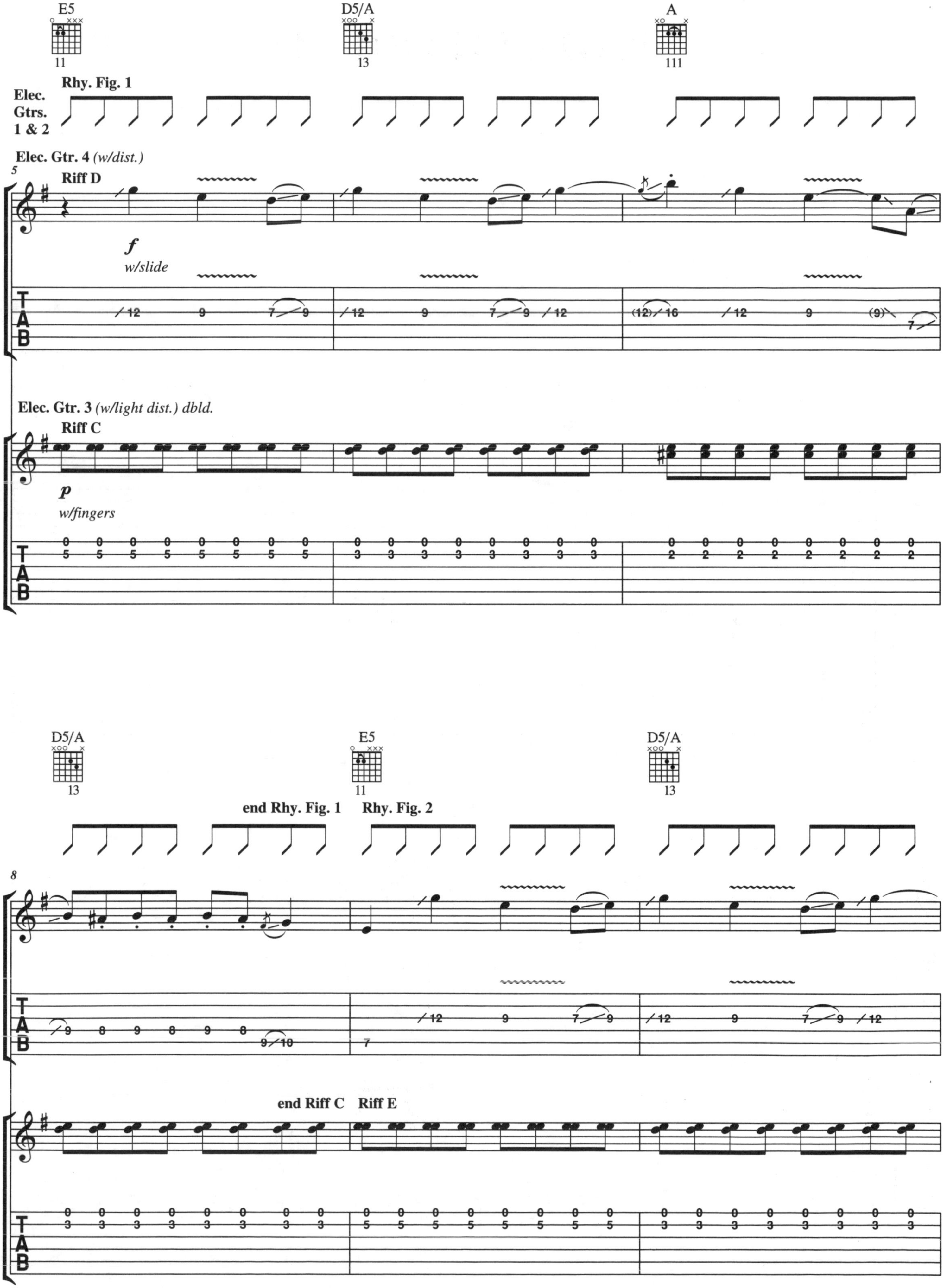
E5
D5/A
A
Rhy. Fig. 1
Elec. Gtrs. 1 & 2
Elec. Gtr. 4 (w/dist.)
Riff D
f
w/slide
Elec. Gtr. 3 (w/light dist.) dbld.
Riff C
p
w/fingers
D5/A
E5
D5/A
end Rhy. Fig. 1
Rhy. Fig. 2
end Riff C
Riff E

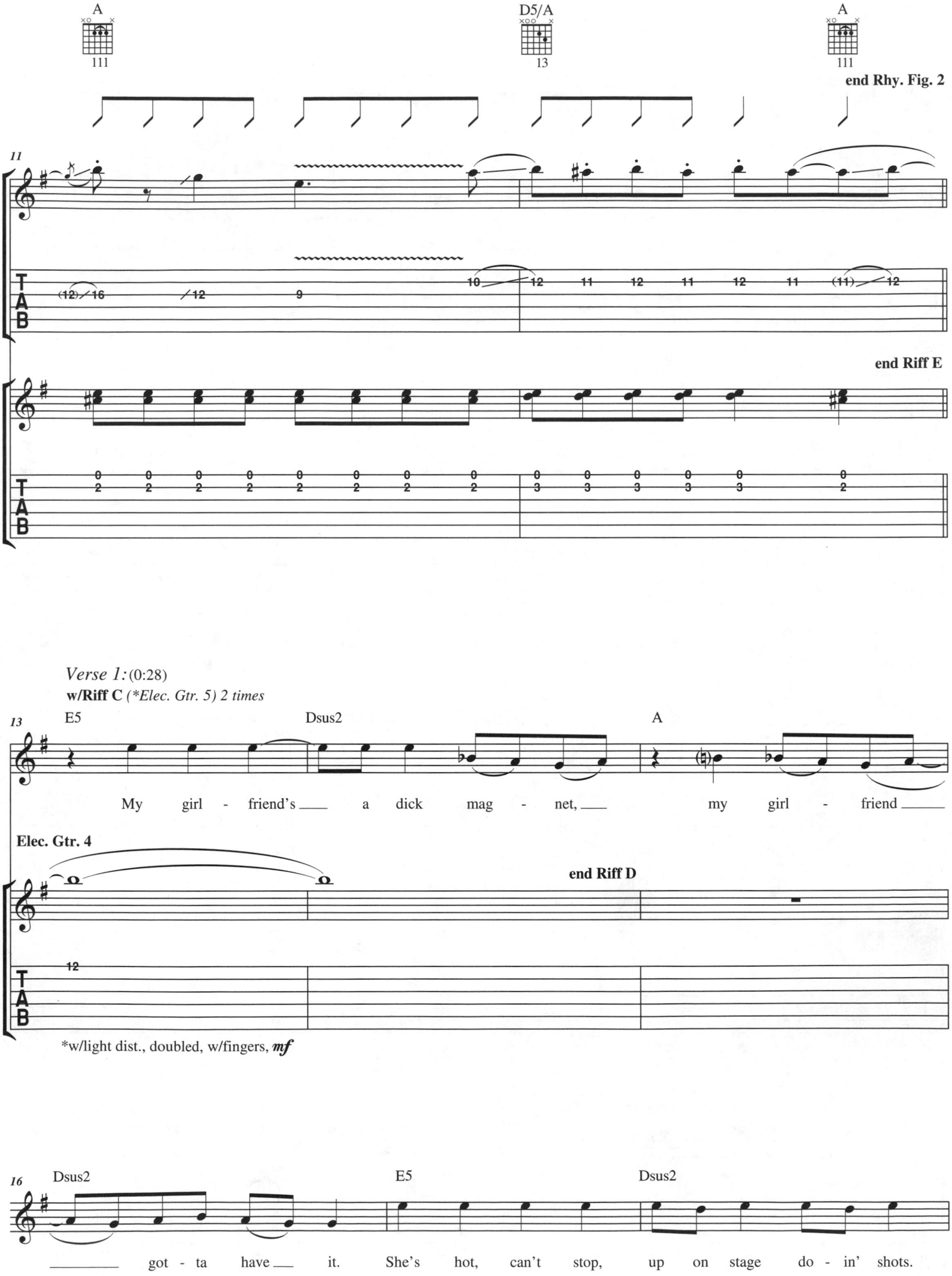
A
D5/A
A
end Rhy. Fig. 2
end Riff E
Verse 1: (0:28)
w/Riff C (*Elec. Gtr. 5) 2 times
E5
Dsus2
A
My girl - friend's a dick mag - net, my girl - friend
Elec. Gtr. 4
end Riff D
*w/light dist., doubled, w/fingers, mf
Dsus2
E5
Dsus2
got - ta have it. She's hot, can't stop, up on stage do - in' shots.

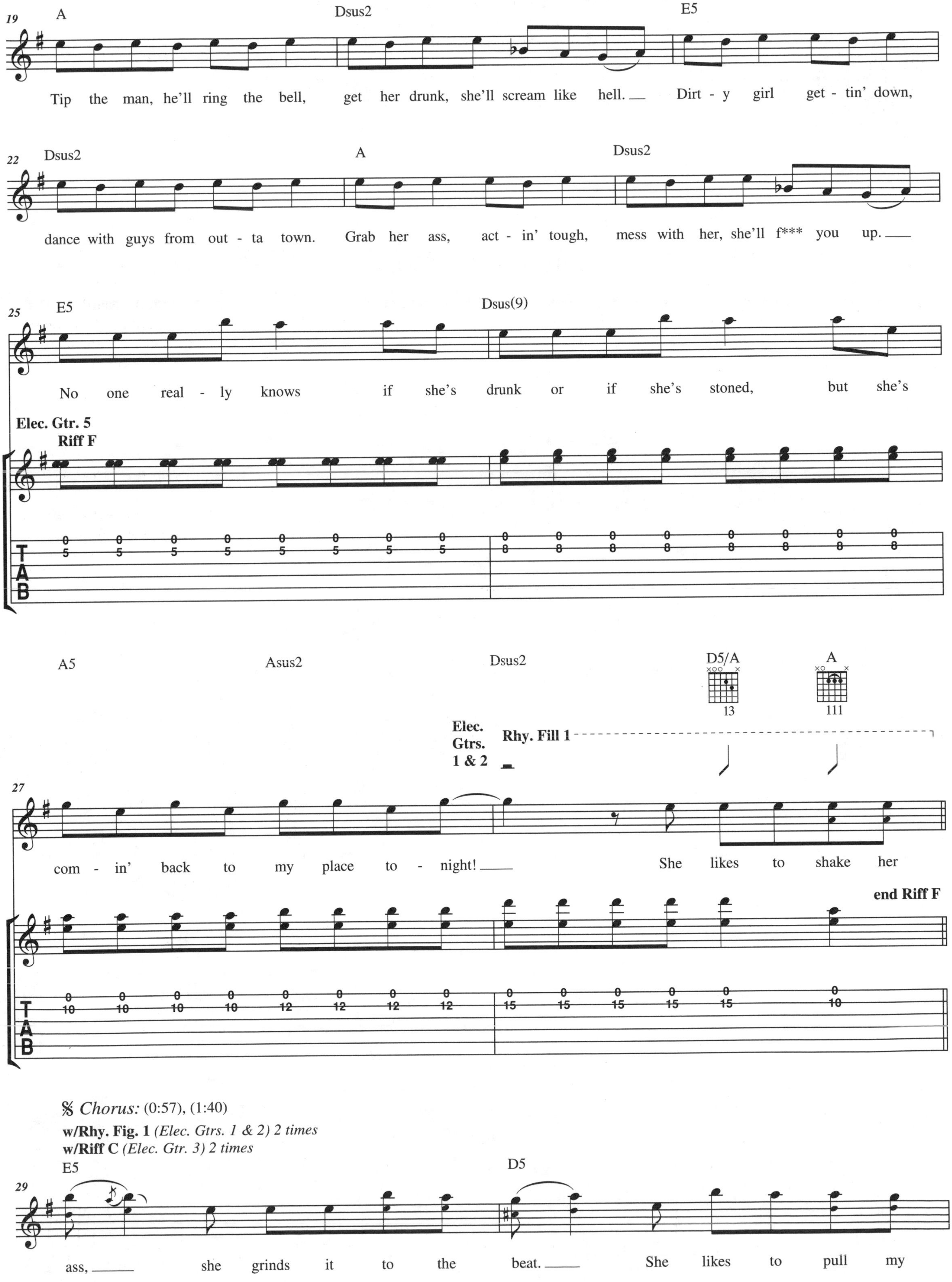
A Dsus2 E5
Tip the man, he'll ring the bell, get her drunk, she'll scream like hell. Dirt - y girl get - tin' down,
Dsus2 A Dsus2
dance with guys from out - ta town. Grab her ass, act - in' tough, mess with her, she'll f*** you up.
E5 Dsus(9)
No one real - ly knows if she's drunk or if she's stoned, but she's
Elec. Gtr. 5
Riff F
A5 Asus2 Dsus2 D5/A A
Elec. Gtrs. 1 & 2
Rhy. Fill 1
com - in' back to my place to - night! She likes to shake her
end Riff F
𝄋 Chorus: (0:57), (1:40)
w/Rhy. Fig. 1 (Elec. Gtrs. 1 & 2) 2 times
w/Riff C (Elec. Gtr. 3) 2 times
E5 D5
ass, she grinds it to the beat. She likes to pull my

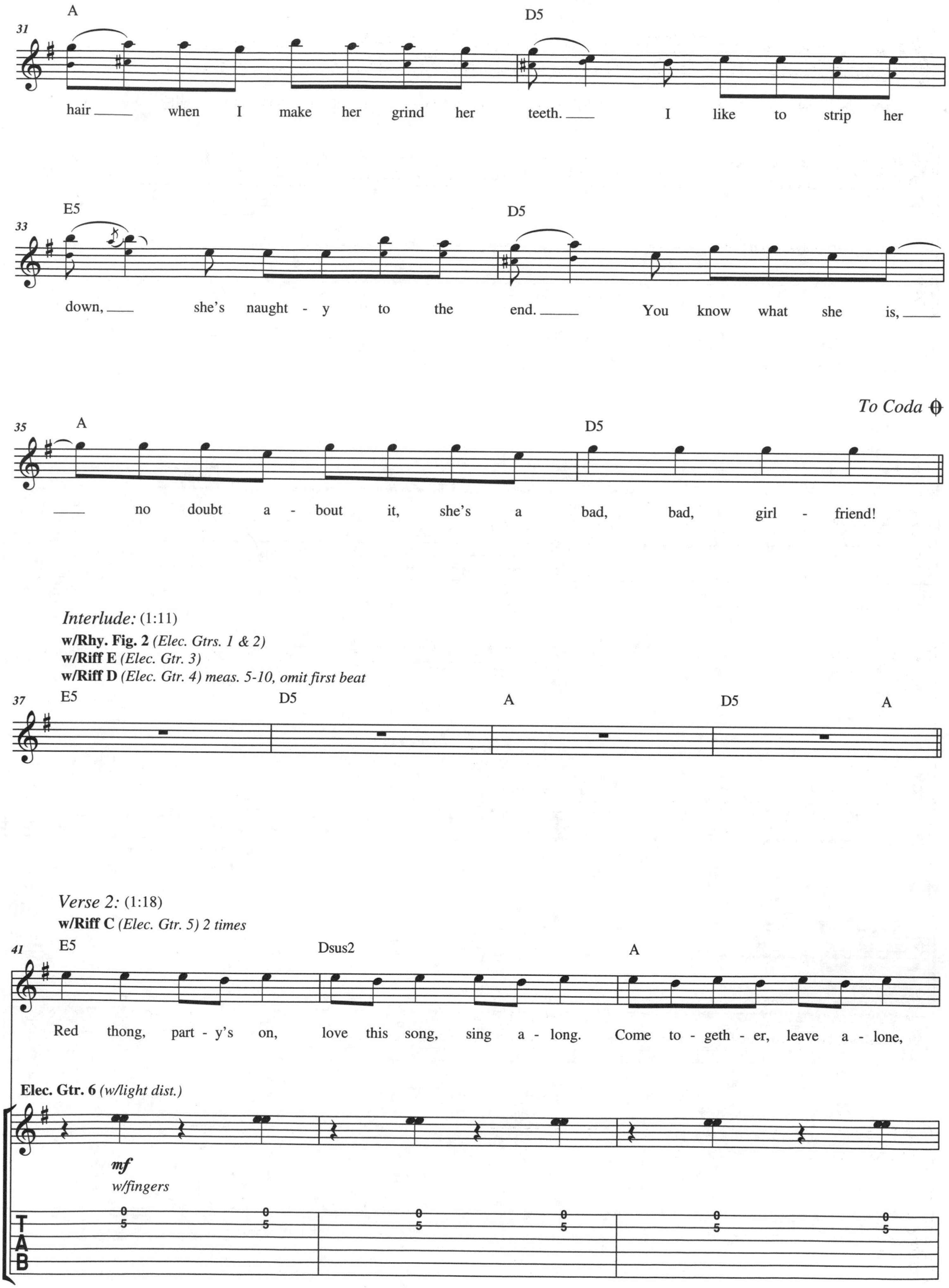
A
D5
31
hair when I make her grind her teeth. I like to strip her
E5
D5
33
down, she's naught - y to the end. You know what she is,
To Coda
A
D5
35
no doubt a - bout it, she's a bad, bad, girl - friend!
Interlude: (1:11)
w/Rhy. Fig. 2 (Elec. Gtrs. 1 & 2)
w/Riff E (Elec. Gtr. 3)
w/Riff D (Elec. Gtr. 4) meas. 5-10, omit first beat
37
E5
D5
A
D5
A
Verse 2: (1:18)
w/Riff C (Elec. Gtr. 5) 2 times
41
E5
Dsus2
A
Red thong, part - y's on, love this song, sing a - long. Come to - geth - er, leave a - lone,
Elec. Gtr. 6 (w/light dist.)
mf
w/fingers

Dsus2
E5
Dsus2
see her lat - er back at home. No - one real - ly knows if she's drunk or if she's stoned but she's
A
Dsus2
w/Riff F (Elec. Gtr. 5)
E5
com - in' back to my place to - night! I say, no one real - ly knows just how
D.S. 𝄋 al Coda
w/Rhy. Fill 1 (Elec. Gtrs. 1 & 2)
Dsus2
A
Dsus2
far she's gon - na go, but I'm gon - na find out lat - er to - night! She likes to shake her

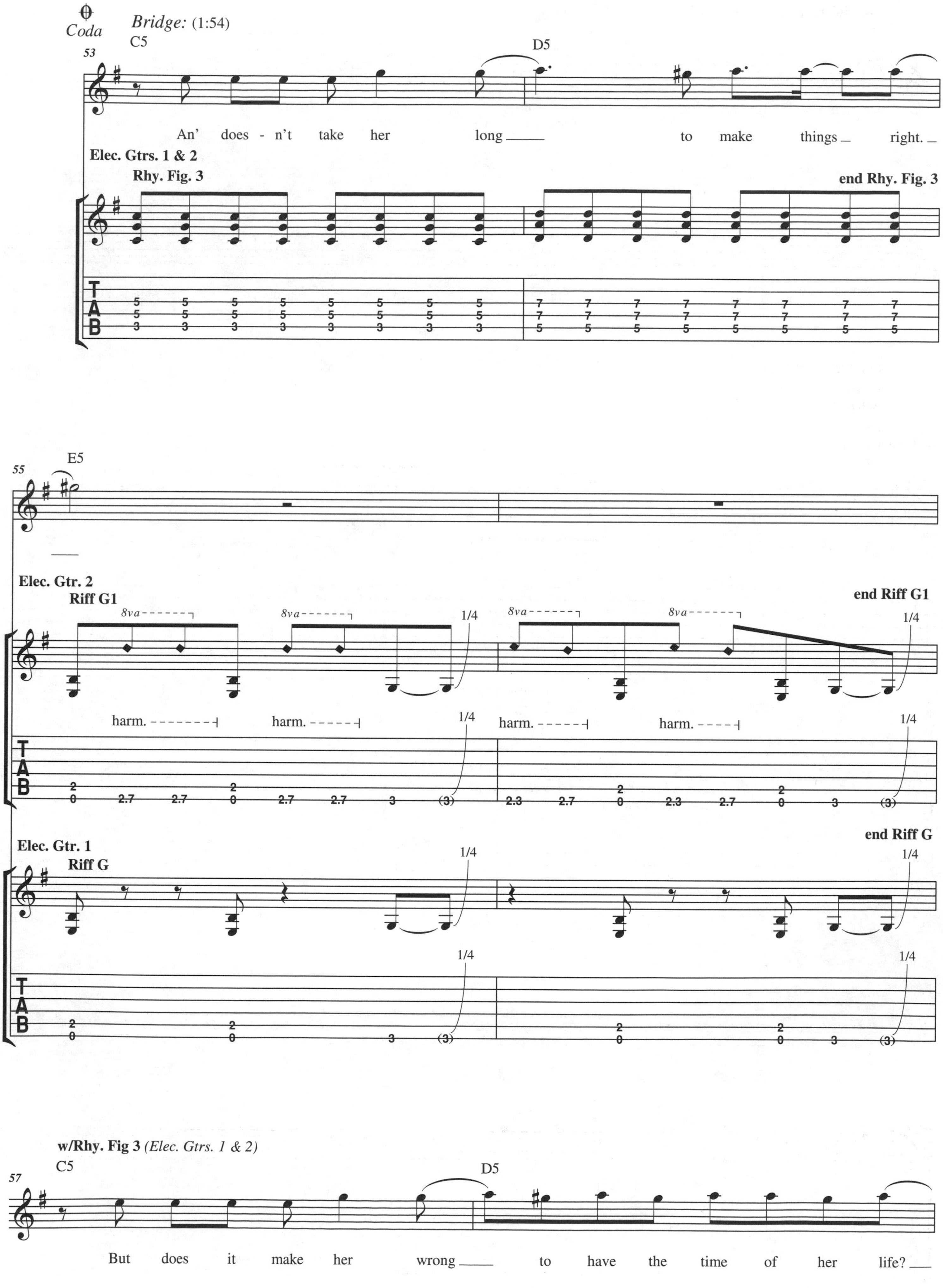
Coda
Bridge: (1:54)
C5
D5
An' does - n't take her long to make things right.
Elec. Gtrs. 1 & 2
Rhy. Fig. 3
end Rhy. Fig. 3
E5
Elec. Gtr. 2
Riff G1
end Riff G1
harm.
Elec. Gtr. 1
Riff G
end Riff G
w/Rhy. Fig 3 (Elec. Gtrs. 1 & 2)
C5
D5
But does it make her wrong to have the time of her life?

w/Riffs G (Elec. Gtr. 1) & G1 (Elec. Gtr. 2) 2 times
E5
59
The time of her life.
w/Riffs A (Elec. Gtr. 1) & A1 (Elec. Gtr. 2) 3 times
w/Riffs B (Elec. Gtr. 1)
& B1 (Elec. Gtr. 2)
63
My girl - friend's a dick mag - net, My girl - friend, got - ta have it.
Guitar Solo: (2:19)
w/Rhy. Fig. 1 (Elec. Gtrs. 1 & 2)
w/Riff C (Elec. Gtr. 3)
E5
D5
A
Elec. Gtr. 6
(w/dist.)
8va
f
1 1/2
1/4
w/Rhy. Fig. 2 (Elec. Gtrs. 1 & 2)
w/Riff E (Elec. Gtr. 3)
D5
E5
D5
73
A
D5
A
She's a
8va

Verse 3: (2:33)
w/Rhy. Fig. 1 (Elec. Gtrs. 1 & 2)
w/Riff C (Elec. Gtr. 3)
75
E5
D5
A
gold dig - ger, now I fig - ured out it's o - ver, pull the trig - ger. Fu - ture's fin - ished, there it went,
(8va)
17
w/Rhy. Fig. 2 (Elec. Gtrs. 1 & 2)
w/Riff E (Elec. Gtr. 3)
78
D5
E5
D5
sav - ings gone, the mon - ey's spent. Look a - round and all I see, no good, bad and ug - ly.
(8va)
81
A
D5
A
N.C.
Man, she's hot and fixed to be the fu - ture ex - Miss Con - nol - ly! She likes to shake her
(8va)
Chorus: (2:49)
w/Rhy. Fig. 1 (Elec. Gtr. 1)
w/Riff C (Elec. Gtr. 3)
84
E5
D5
A
ass, she grinds it to the beat. She likes to pull my hair when I make her grind her

w/Rhy. Fig. 2 (Elec. Gtrs. 1 & 2)
w/Riff E (Elec. Gtr. 3)
D5
E5
D5
teeth. I like to strip her down, she's naught - y to the end. You know what she is
Outro: (3:03)
w/Rhy. Fig. 1 (Elec. Gtrs. 1 & 2)
w/Riff C (Elec. Gtr. 3)
w/Riff D (Elec. Gtr. 4) first 8 meas.
A
D5
A
E5
no doubt a - bout it, she's a bad, bad, girl - friend!
w/Rhy. Fig. 2 (Elec. Gtrs. 1 & 2)
w/Riff E (Elec. Gtr. 3)
D5
A
D5
E5
She's a bad, bad, girl - friend!
D5
A
D5
A
She's a bad, bad, girl - friend!
E5
Elec. Gtr. 2
Elec. Gtr. 1

HATE MY LIFE

Lyrics by TYLER CONNOLLY and CHRISTINE CONNOLLY
Music by TYLER CONNOLLY, DAVID BRENNER
and DEAN BACK

*All Gtrs. tune down 1/2 step:

⑥ = E♭ ③ = G♭
⑤ = A♭ ② = B♭
④ = D♭ ① = E♭

Moderately ♩ = 112

Verse 1: (0:02)

D
132
Elec. Gtr. 1
(clean-tone)
mf
grad. accel. next 16 meas.
So sick of the ho - bos
al - ways beg - gin' for change.

*Recording sounds a half step lower than written.

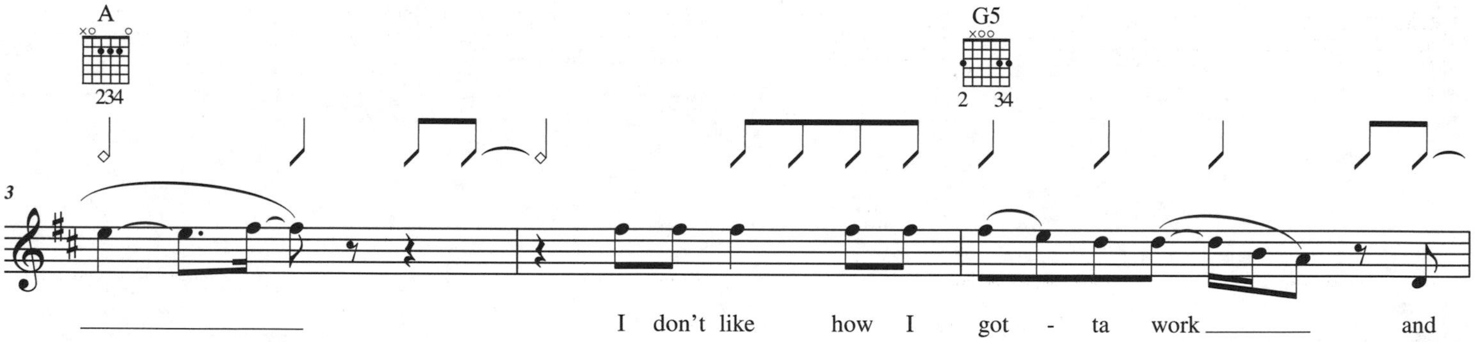
A
234
G5
2 34
3
I don't like how I got - ta work and

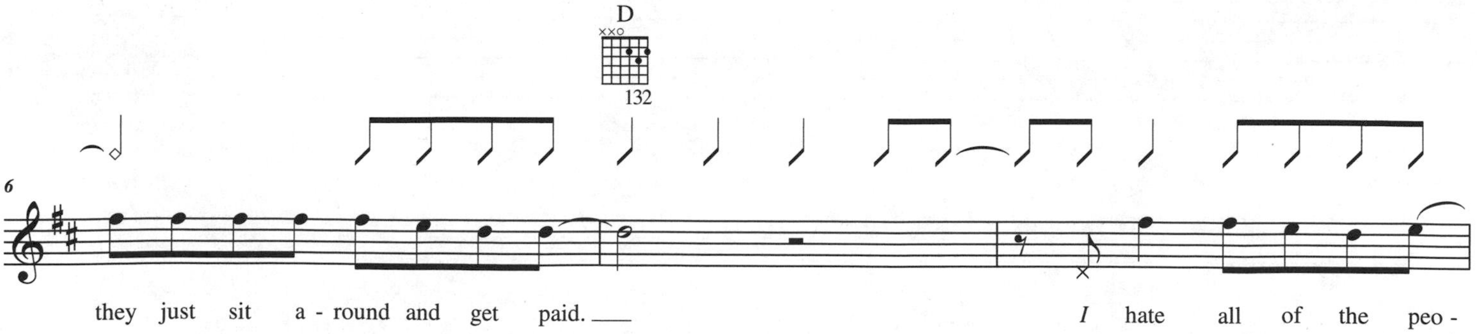
D
132
6
they just sit a - round and get paid.
I hate all of the peo -

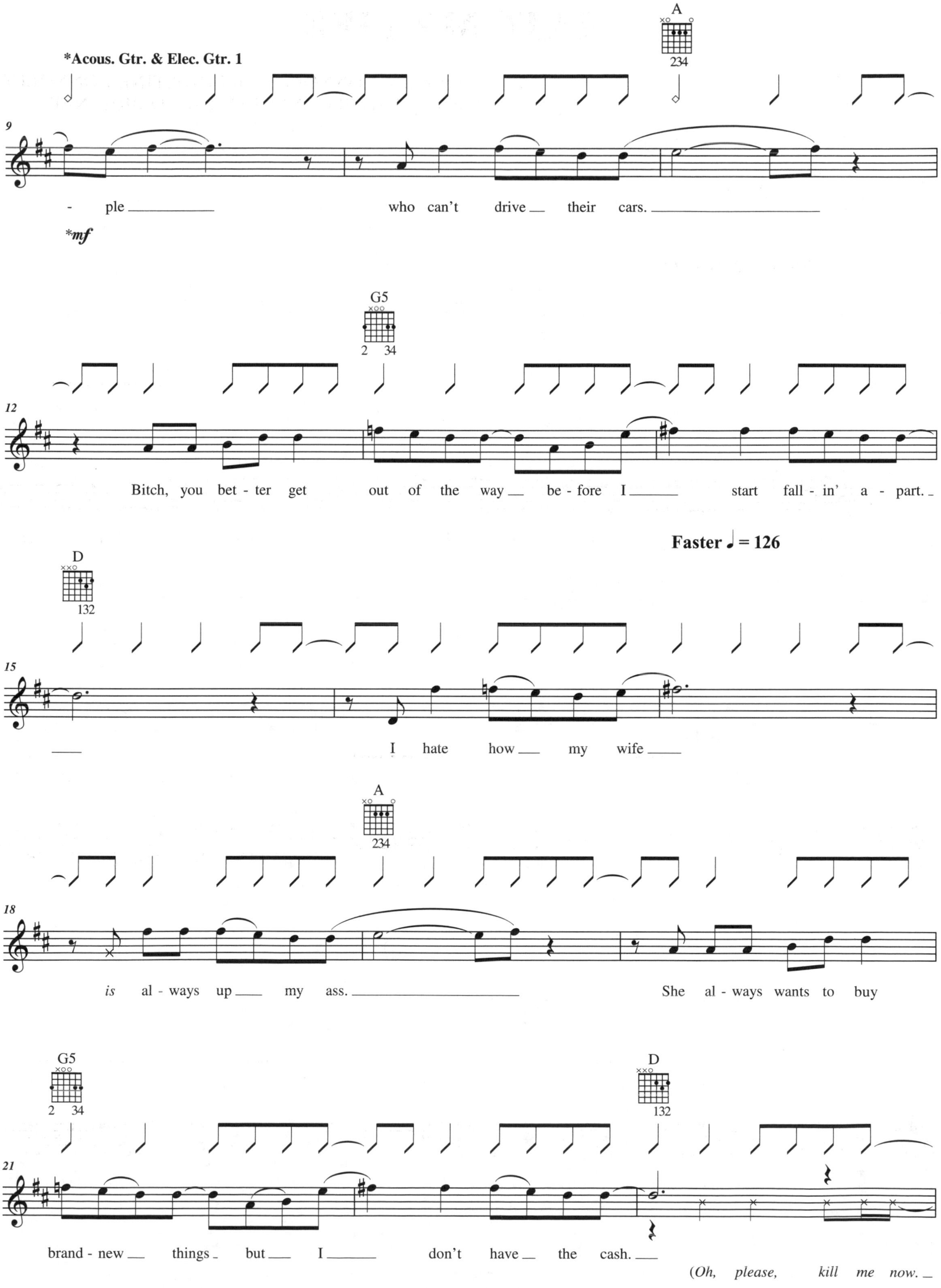
*Acous. Gtr. & Elec. Gtr. 1
A
234
- ple who can't drive their cars.
*mf
G5
2 34
Bitch, you bet - ter get out of the way be - fore I start fall - in' a - part.
D
132
Faster ♩ = 126
I hate how my wife
A
234
is al - ways up my ass. She al - ways wants to buy
G5
2 34
D
132
brand - new things but I don't have the cash.
(Oh, please, kill me now.

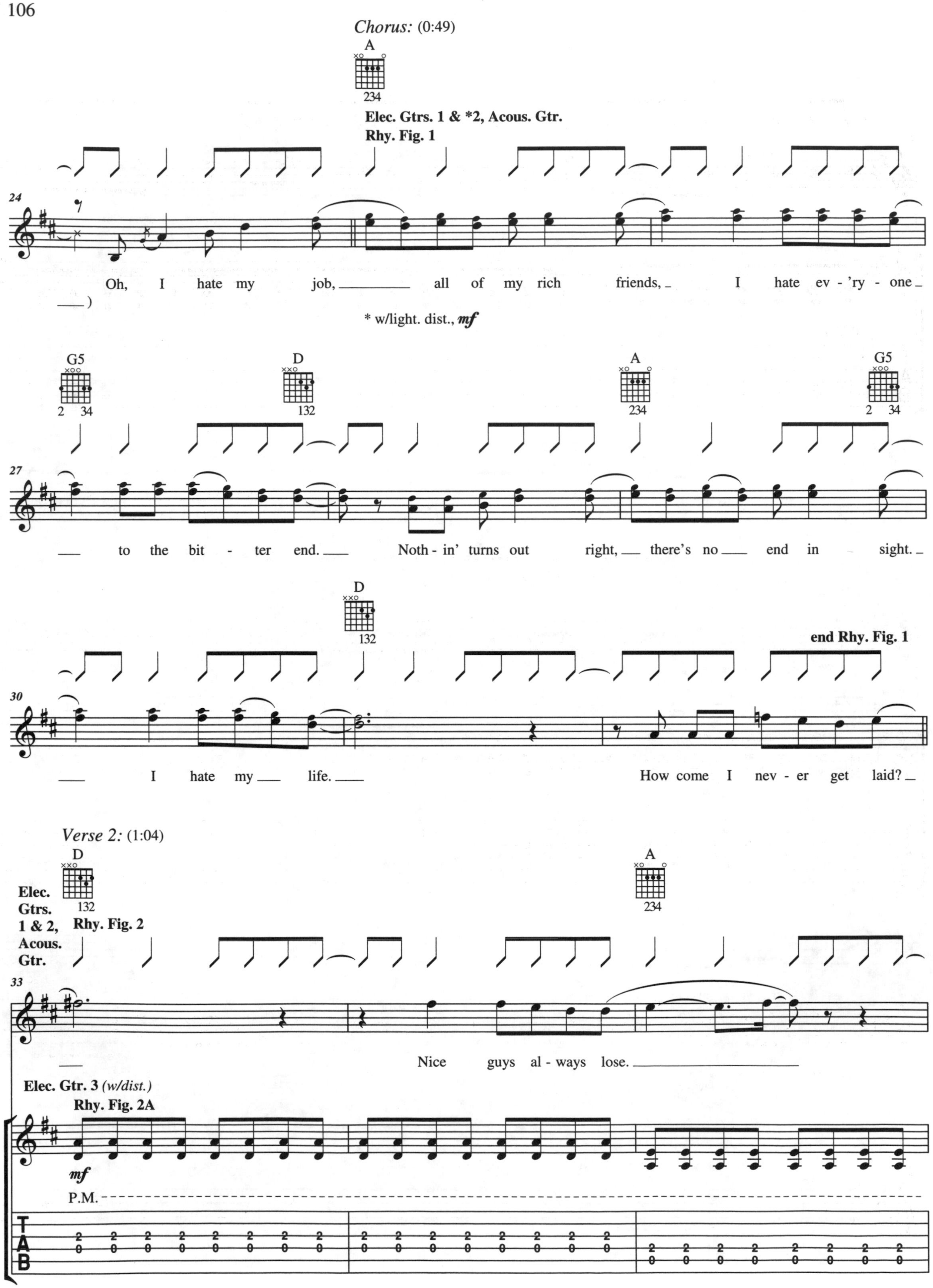
Chorus: (0:49)
A
Elec. Gtrs. 1 & *2, Acous. Gtr.
Rhy. Fig. 1
Oh, I hate my job, all of my rich friends, I hate ev - 'ry - one
* w/light. dist., mf
G5
D
A
G5
to the bit - ter end. Noth - in' turns out right, there's no end in sight.
D
end Rhy. Fig. 1
I hate my life. How come I nev - er get laid?
Verse 2: (1:04)
D
A
Elec. Gtrs. 1 & 2, Acous. Gtr.
Rhy. Fig. 2
Nice guys al - ways lose.
Elec. Gtr. 3 (w/dist.)
Rhy. Fig. 2A
mf
P.M.

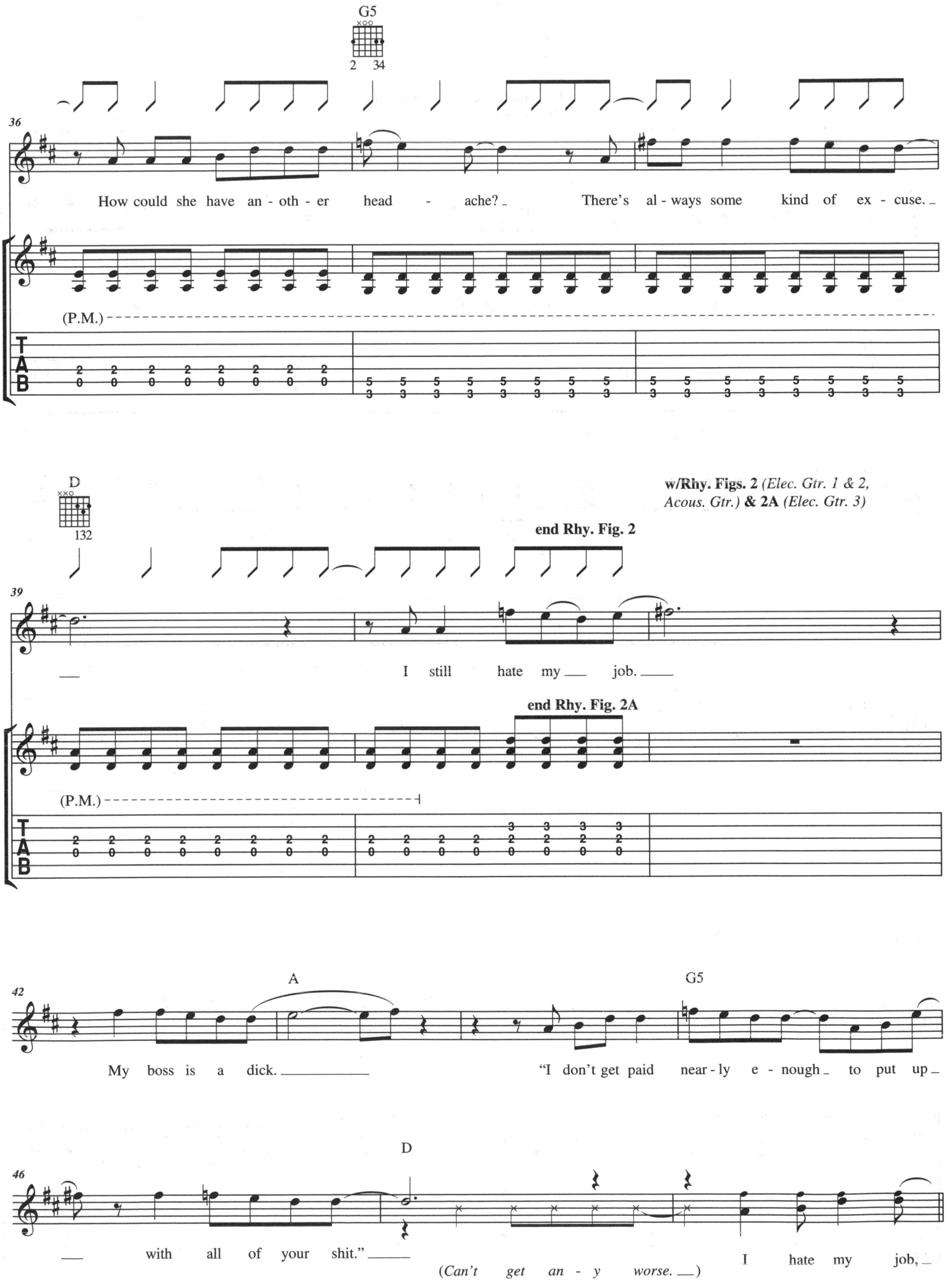
G5
How could she have an - oth - er head - ache? There's al - ways some kind of ex - cuse.
(P.M.)
D
w/Rhy. Figs. 2 (Elec. Gtr. 1 & 2, Acous. Gtr.) & 2A (Elec. Gtr. 3)
end Rhy. Fig. 2
I still hate my job.
end Rhy. Fig. 2A
(P.M.)
A
G5
My boss is a dick. "I don't get paid near - ly e - nough to put up
D
with all of your shit."
(Can't get an - y worse.)
I hate my job,

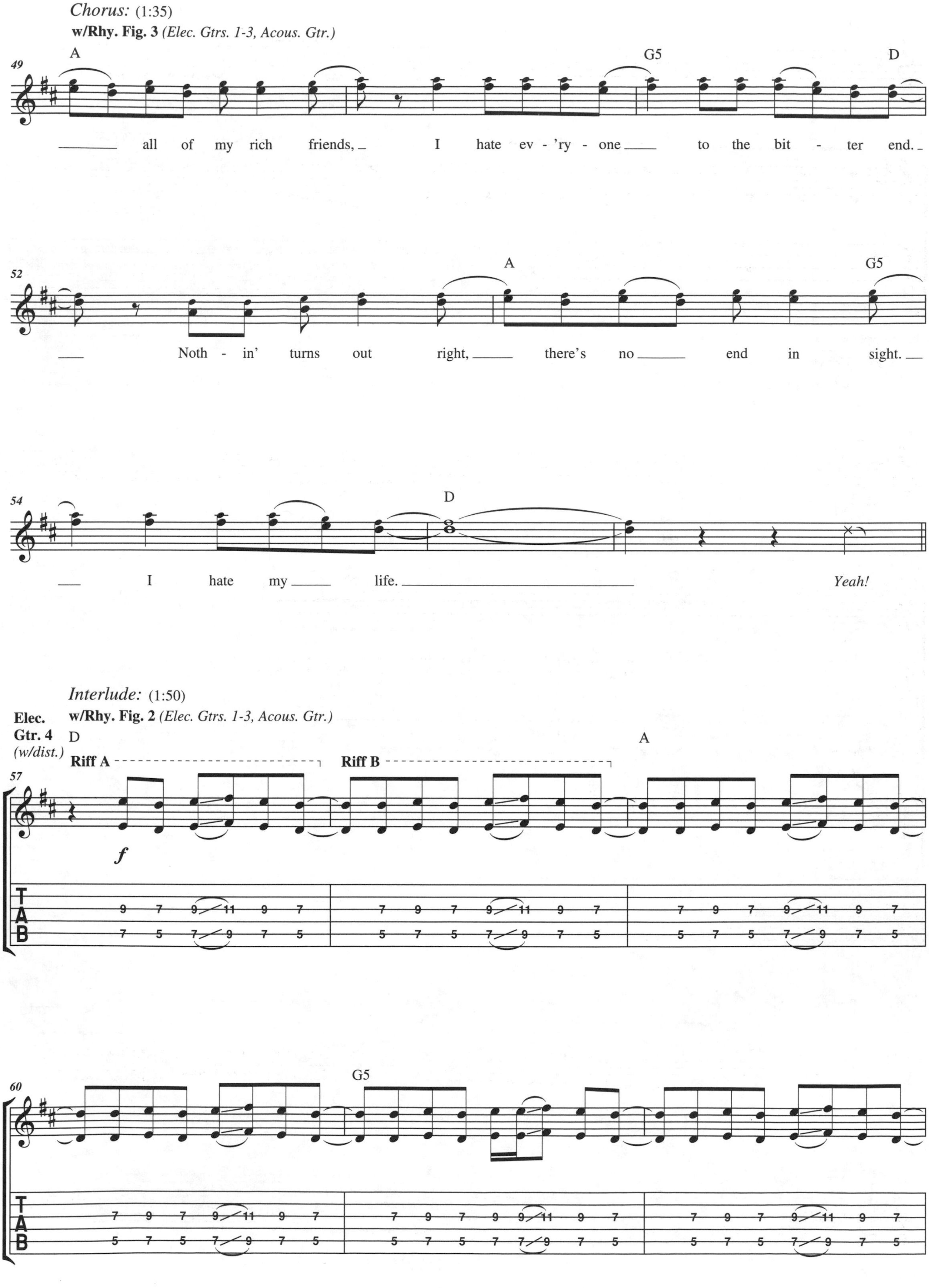
Chorus: (1:35)
w/Rhy. Fig. 3 (Elec. Gtrs. 1-3, Acous. Gtr.)
49
A
G5
D
all of my rich friends, I hate ev - 'ry - one to the bit - ter end.
52
A
G5
Noth - in' turns out right, there's no end in sight.
54
D
I hate my life.
Yeah!
Interlude: (1:50)
w/Rhy. Fig. 2 (Elec. Gtrs. 1-3, Acous. Gtr.)
Elec. Gtr. 4 (w/dist.)
D
A
Riff A
Riff B
57
f
T
A
B
9 7 9 11 9 7
7 5 7 9 7 5
7 9 7 9 11 9 7
5 7 5 7 9 7 5
7 9 7 9 11 9 7
5 7 5 7 9 7 5
60
G5
7 9 7 9 11 9 7
5 7 5 7 9 7 5
7 9 7 9 9 11 9 7
5 7 5 7 7 9 7 5
7 9 7 9 11 9 7
5 7 5 7 9 7 5

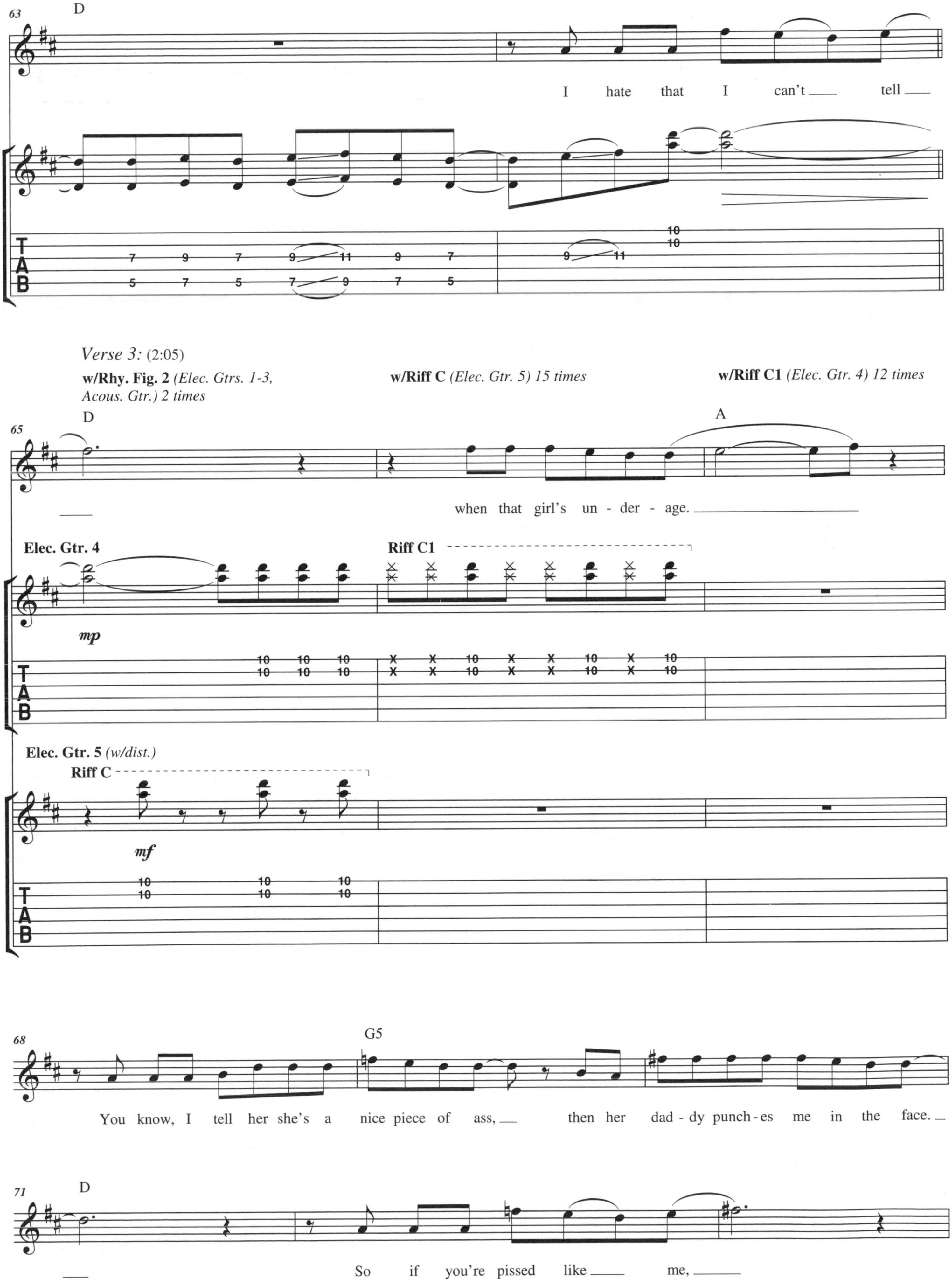
63
D
I hate that I can't tell
Verse 3: (2:05)
w/Rhy. Fig. 2 (Elec. Gtrs. 1-3, Acous. Gtr.) 2 times
w/Riff C (Elec. Gtr. 5) 15 times
w/Riff C1 (Elec. Gtr. 4) 12 times
65
D
A
when that girl's un - der - age.
Elec. Gtr. 4
Riff C1
mp
Elec. Gtr. 5 (w/dist.)
Riff C
mf
68
G5
You know, I tell her she's a nice piece of ass, then her dad - dy punch - es me in the face.
71
D
So if you're pissed like me,

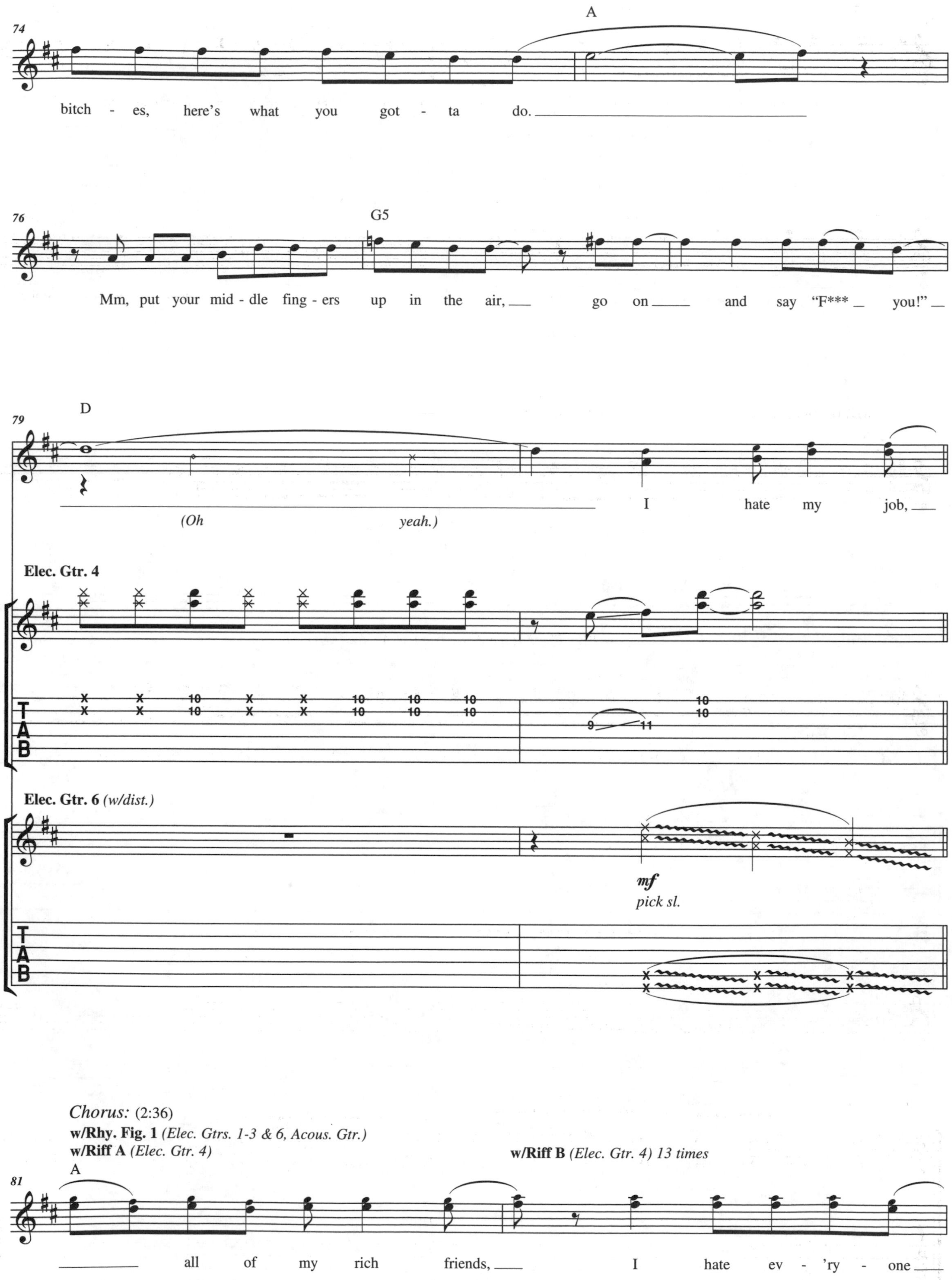
74
A
bitch - es, here's what you got - ta do.
76
G5
Mm, put your mid - dle fing - ers up in the air, go on and say "F*** you!"
79
D
(Oh yeah.)
I hate my job,
Elec. Gtr. 4
Elec. Gtr. 6 (w/dist.)
mf
pick sl.
Chorus: (2:36)
w/Rhy. Fig. 1 (Elec. Gtrs. 1-3 & 6, Acous. Gtr.)
w/Riff A (Elec. Gtr. 4)
w/Riff B (Elec. Gtr. 4) 13 times
81
A
all of my rich friends, I hate ev - 'ry - one

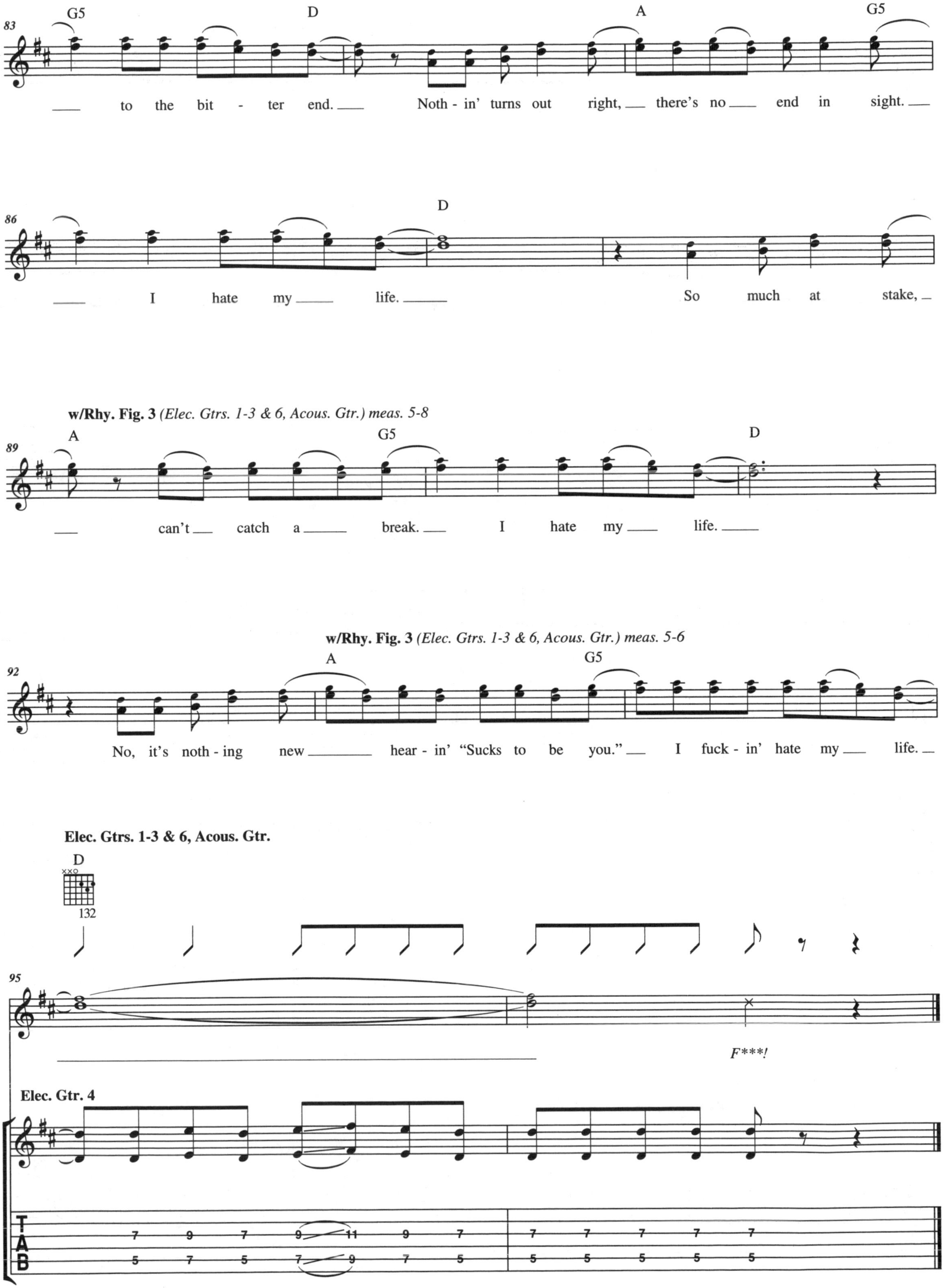
83
G5
D
A
G5
to the bit - ter end. Noth - in' turns out right, there's no end in sight.
86
D
I hate my life. So much at stake,
w/Rhy. Fig. 3 (Elec. Gtrs. 1-3 & 6, Acous. Gtr.) meas. 5-8
89
A
G5
D
can't catch a break. I hate my life.
w/Rhy. Fig. 3 (Elec. Gtrs. 1-3 & 6, Acous. Gtr.) meas. 5-6
92
A
G5
No, it's noth - ing new hear - in' "Sucks to be you." I fuck - in' hate my life.
Elec. Gtrs. 1-3 & 6, Acous. Gtr.
D
132
95
F***!
Elec. Gtr. 4
T
A
B
7 9 7 9 11 9 7
5 7 5 7 9 7 5
7 7 7 7 7
5 5 5 5 5

GUITAR TAB GLOSSARY

TABLATURE EXPLANATION

TAB illustrates the six strings of the guitar.
Notes and chords are indicated by the placement of fret numbers on each string.

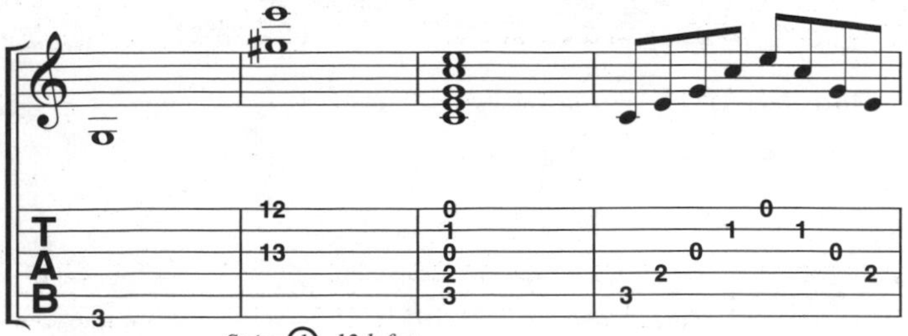

String ⑥, 3rd fret — *String ①, 12th fret / String ③, 13th fret* — *A "C" chord* — *C chord arpeggiated*

BENDING NOTES

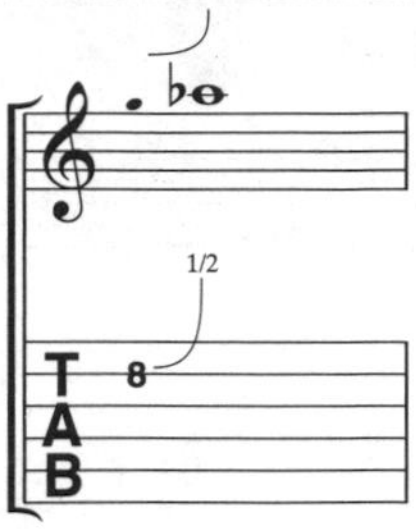

Half Step: Play the note and bend string one half step (one fret).

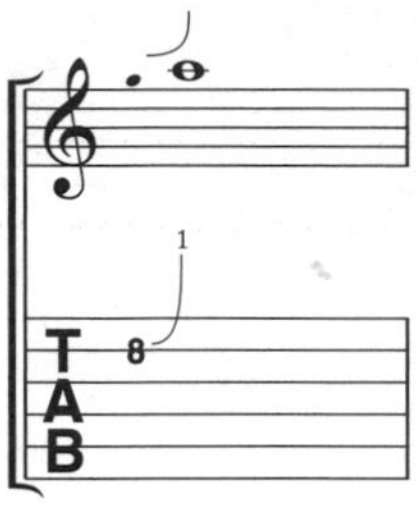

Whole Step: Play the note and bend string one whole step (two frets).

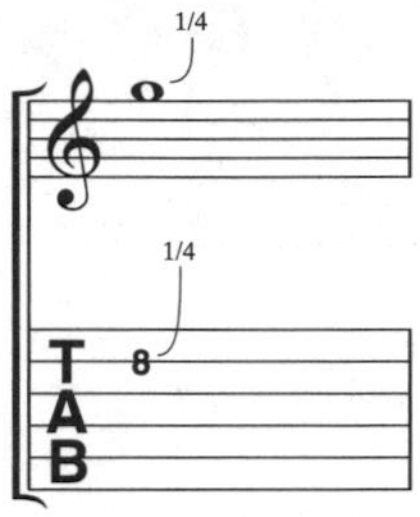

Slight Bend/ Quarter-Tone Bend: Play the note and bend string sharp.

Prebend and Release: Play the already-bent string, then immediately drop it down to the fretted note.

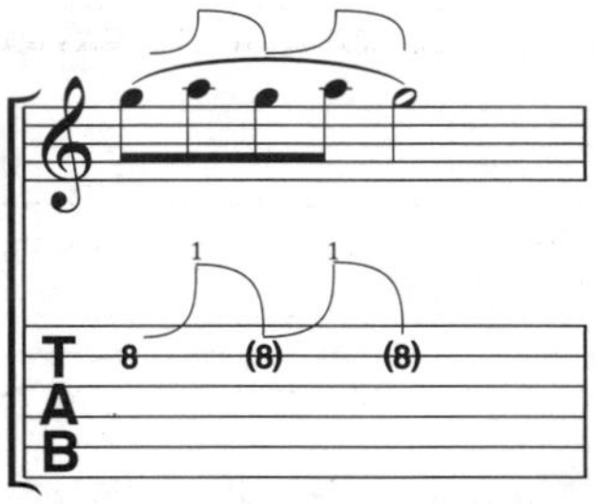

Bend and Release: Play the note and bend to the next pitch, then release to the original note. Only the first note is attacked.

PICK DIRECTION

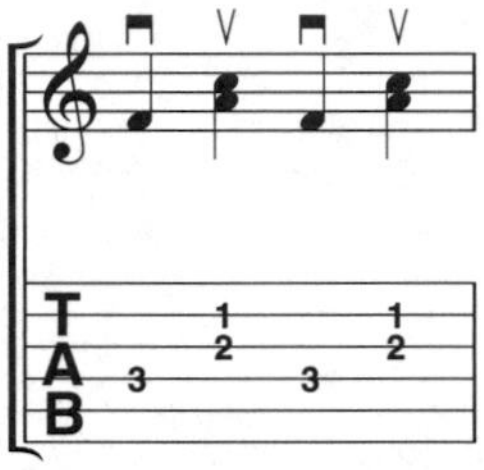

Downstrokes and Upstrokes: The downstroke is indicated with this symbol (⊓) and the upstroke is indicated with this (V).

ARTICULATIONS

Hammer On: Play the lower note, then "hammer" your finger to the higher note. Only the first note is plucked.

Pull Off: Play the higher note with your first finger already in position on the lower note. Pull your finger off the first note with a strong downward motion that plucks the string—sounding the lower note.

Palm Mute: The notes are muted (muffled) by placing the palm of the pick hand lightly on the strings, just in front of the bridge.

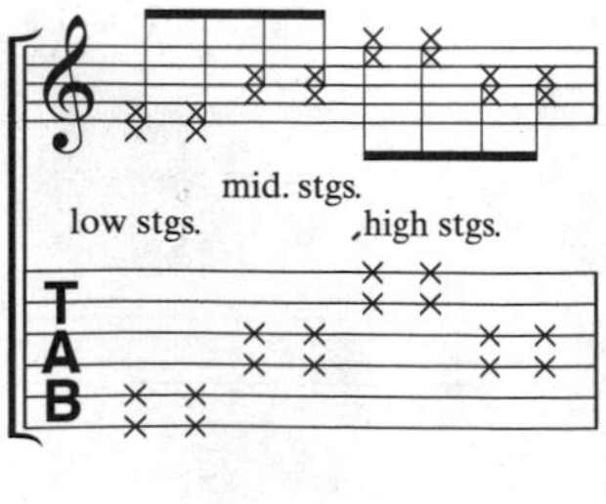

Muted Strings: A percussive sound is produced by striking the strings while laying the fret hand across them.

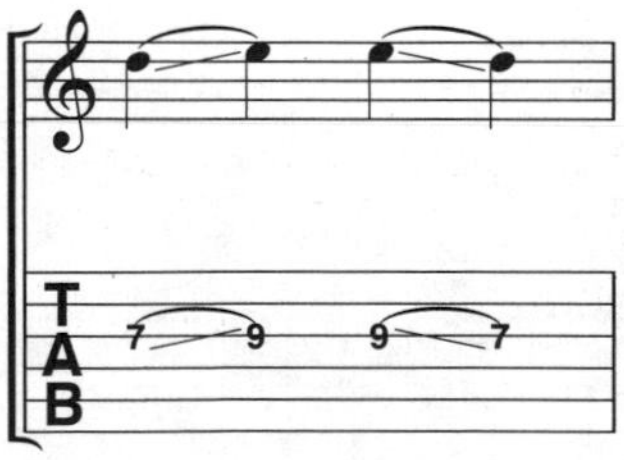

Legato Slide: Play the first note and, keeping pressure applied on the string, slide up to the second note. The diagonal line shows that it is a slide and not a hammer-on or a pull-off.

HARMONICS

Natural Harmonic: A finger of the fret hand lightly touches the string at the note indicated in the TAB and is plucked by the pick producing a bell-like sound called a harmonic.

Artificial Harmonic: Fret the note at the first TAB number, lightly touch the string at the fret indicated in parens (usually 12 frets higher than the fretted note), then pluck the string with an available finger or your pick.

RHYTHM SLASHES

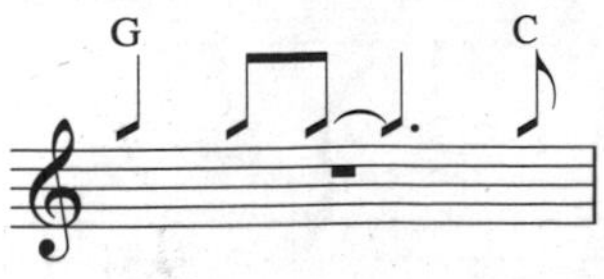

Strum Marks/ Rhythm Slashes: Strum with the indicated rhythm pattern. Strum marks can be located above the staff or within the staff.

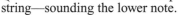

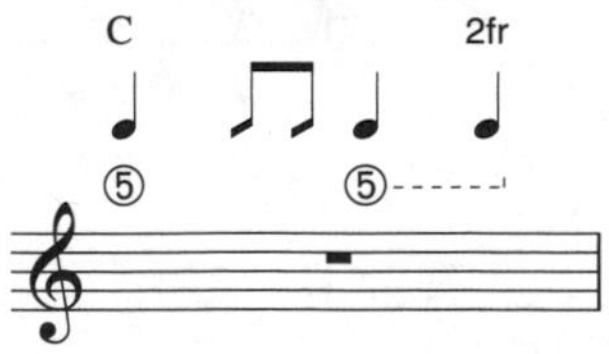

Single Notes with Rhythm Slashes: Sometimes single notes are incorporated into a strum pattern. The circled number below is the string and the fret number is above.